1982

THE EDUCATION
OF DEAF CHILDREN

A University Park Press
Topicbook

The University Park Press **Topicbooks** are carefully selected, written, and designed to identify the issues and controversies in communication science and disorders, to help readers find their way through the broad range of information available, and to serve as short topical introductions for professionals and students.

THE EDUCATION OF DEAF CHILDREN
Issues, Theory, and Practice

STEPHEN P. QUIGLEY, PH.D.
Professor of Education and Speech and Hearing Science
University of Illinois at Urbana-Champaign

ROBERT E. KRETSCHMER, PH.D.
Associate Professor of Special Education
Teachers College, Columbia University

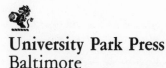

University Park Press
Baltimore

UNIVERSITY PARK PRESS
International Publishers in Science, Medicine, and Education
300 North Charles Street
Baltimore, Maryland 21201

Copyright©1982 by University Park Press

Typeset by Britton Composition

Manufactured in the United States of America by The Maple Press Company

Library of Congress Cataloging in Publication Data
Quigley, Stephen Patrick, 1927–
The education of deaf children.
Bibliography: p. 111
Includes index.
1. Deaf—Education.   2. Children, Deaf.
I. Kretschmer, Robert E.   II. Title.
HV2430.Q5   371.91'2   81-21840
ISBN 0-8391-1711-6   AACR2

CONTENTS

Preface to **Fundamentals of Communication
Science** vii

Preface ix

1 Definitions and Educational Programs 1
2 Language and Communication Methods 9
3 Learning Environments 31
4 Cognitive and Intellectual Development 49
5 Reading, Written Language, and Academic Achievement 65
6 Social, Affective, and Occupational Aspects of Deafness 87
7 Some Summary and Concluding Remarks 103

References 111

Index 123

PREFACE
to Fundamentals of Communication Science

The publication of **Fundamentals of Communication Science** is undertaken with several purposes in mind. A primary objective is to produce a series of short, carefully prepared, scientifically sound, and clearly written introductory-level books concerning speech, hearing, and language. Each book is intended to address theoretical issues and/or empirical data which experts agree are the fundamental ideas and relations that define a particular area of knowledge. Each book is intended for a number of different courses taught in one or more departments in most colleges and universities.

Above all, we hope to contribute a series of useful and interesting books that will introduce undergraduate students to nationally known scholars who normally write original articles and evaluative reviews oriented toward other professionals and graduate students.

Constantine Trahiotis, Ph.D.
Charles E. Speaks, Ph.D.
Series Editors

PREFACE

This small volume was written to provide 1) a concise factual base of information on the education of deaf children and youth, 2) discussions of several enduring issues in the field, 3) a representative sampling of research on those issues, and 4) some conclusions concerning the issues drawn on the basis of available evidence. Thus, the book is primarily issues oriented, with sufficient factual information on the education of deaf children and youth being supplied to provide for an understanding of the issues. The issues treated are those about which any person seeking to understand the field or seeking to work with deaf people must eventually form an opinion. Although the book is subtitled "Issues, Theory, and Practice," not much is said about practice because of space limitations. We left the word in the title, however, because some aspects of practice that relate to important issues are dealt with in the text.

Having stated what we believe the book is, let us state what it is not. It is not a comprehensive text on the education of deaf children and youth. Several good texts of that nature already exist [e.g., Davis and Silverman (1978) and Moores (1978)]. It also is not a treatise for any particular position on educating deaf children and youth. A number of those texts also exist, and the education of deaf children and youth has usually been dominated throughout its long history by one or another passionately held point of view. We do not belittle any points of view, people who hold them, or texts that espouse them. The education of a truly prelingually deaf child is so incredibly difficult, and observable progress so slow, that any teacher must inevitably have a strongly held belief in his/her educational position and

ix

practices to be able to return to the classroom day after day. However, we believe sufficient research data are now available to allow for a more reasoned examination and discussion of the issues than has heretofore been possible. That is what this book attempts to do.

The book consists of seven chapters, most of which deal with what the authors consider to be important and enduring issues in the education of deaf children and youth. Each chapter usually contains a description of the issue, background information concerning it, presentation of research evidence concerning it, and some conclusions (usually appropriately tentative) reached by the authors on the basis of the evidence—inevitably filtered through our own viewpoints, which are stated briefly. Chapter 1 contains some basic information on measurement, etiology, and incidence of hearing impairment and on educational programs for deaf children and youth. In Chapter 2 we deal with what we consider to be the central issue in the education of deaf children and youth—the educational effectiveness of various types of communication methods. Chapter 3 is concerned with a second educational issue: the influence of different learning environments (home and type of school placement) on various aspects of development. Chapter 4 presents basic information on cognitive and intellectual development and treats the issue of whether development of those capacities in deaf children proceeds at the same pace and in the same manner as for hearing children. Reading, written language, and educational achievement are covered in Chapter 5 along with the critical issue of whether successful development of reading can take place without a pre-established, internal auditory-based language. In Chapter 6, personal and social adjustment and occupational status are treated in the context of the issue of whether prelingual deafness imposes certain patterns of personal and social behavior or whether such behavior is an indirect result of deafness. Chapter 7 is a brief summary.

We have departed from usual practice in brief general survey texts by basing most of the presentation in each chapter on specific research studies. For each important issue we have presented many of the major research studies relating to it, have discussed the studies, and have drawn some conclusions from them. As stated at appropriate places in the text, conclusions made are usually tentative, because they often are based on only one or a few studies. The studies are presented nontechnically and in enough detail for the general reader to make some evaluation of them, and the original sources are cited for more detailed study.

This research-based approach was deliberate. Some of the issues in the education of deaf children are highly charged with emotion, especially the issue of the form of communication to be used by and with the children. The issues also, until the past two decades, have been little illuminated by research. The accumulation of research in recent years, however, has made possible the present approach.

Some selectivity had to be exercised in the research studies presented because of the nature of the book and limitations on space. Mostly, we followed the traditions of research by giving priority in selection to those studies that have undergone peer evaluation for publication in refereed professional journals or for acceptance as doctoral dissertations. We also included some nonrefereed publications when we considered their inclusion to be important, but for the most part such publications were not included.

As stated, the views of the authors probably, and inevitably, have filtered the data presented and discussed — even though we believe those views were formed from lengthy and judicious consideration of the evidence. We will state the relevant viewpoints so that the reader can be aware (and wary) of them while reading the book. There are just two.

1. The primary goal of education for typical (non–multiply handicapped) prelingually deaf children should be literacy — the ability to read and write at a mature level the general language of society, which in the United States is English. Where multiple handicaps or other complicating factors added to deafness make mature literacy genuinely unrealistic, occupational self-sufficiency is a reasonable substitute goal.

2. Development of the deaf child's (and, in fact, of any child's) educational potential requires an early environment that provides a wealth of stimulating and relevant learning experiences that are made meaningful for the child through interaction with other people by means of a fluent and intelligible communication system. Fluent communication is particularly important in infancy and early childhood when the parents or parent surrogates are the principal figures in the child's life.

We believe these two statements relate directly to most major educational issues in the education of deaf children and to most important educational goals. For example, reading is an indispensable tool for mastering all academic subject matter (although an important dissenting view is presented in Chapter 5). Mastery of reading, however, seems to depend on a pre-established, internalized language system that, in turn, seems to be a direct product of a stimulating early environment and fluent and intelligible communication between child and parents.

In a similar manner, other major educational questions can be related to our two statements. We have used reading as an example because we believe it should be a primary concern in educating deaf children. It also is likely that reading will be a major area for research during the next decade or more in the education of deaf children and youth. A primary focus in the research on reading development is likely to be the relationship of various internalized language systems, and the communication systems on which they are based, to elements of the reading process.

This book is possible at this time because of the explosion of research in the education of deaf children and youth that has taken place during the past two decades. The education of deaf children and youth shared in the great expansion of educational programs of all types that took place during the late 1950s and the 1960s. A notable result of that great expansion in education, and in the social sciences related to it, was an influx of psychologists, psycholinguists, and linguists into language, cognitive, and personal and social adjustment research with deaf individuals. This fortunate involvement of various disciplines in research on the language and cognitive development of deaf people has influenced educational theory and practice, as has the recent research of people more directly identified with the education of deaf children and youth. The work of all those individuals during the past 20 years has made this book possible.

In addition to a generalized debt of gratitude to all the researchers and others who contributed the work on which this book is based, we owe specific thanks to a number of people. First, we are indebted to several of our doctoral students who aided in reviewing a large literature of which we have been able to report only a sampling. Doctoral candidates are unsung, underpaid, and overworked (but not always, as they often believe, unappreciated) essentials in the university research process. We express our gratitude to these graduate students, in alphabetical order: Jean Andrews, Cynthia King, John-Allen Payne, Marilyn Salter, and Pam Stuckey. Deep appreciation is due also to our wives, Carol Kretschmer and Ruth Quigley, who, like many academic wives, were pressed into service in proofreading, draft typing, bibliography preparation, and many other tedious but vital tasks involved in manuscript preparation. Finally, we express our thanks to that other underpaid, overworked, and unsung (but, again, not unappreciated) essential of the university research process—the secretary. In our case this was Carol Goering, who patiently and expertly transformed the chicken scratches, misspellings, incomplete sentences, and incoherent paragraphs of the authors into a coherent manuscript.

Stephen P. Quigley
Robert E. Kretschmer

For Ruth and Carol and Phil and Stephanie

THE EDUCATION
OF DEAF CHILDREN

1

DEFINITIONS AND EDUCATIONAL PROGRAMS

Because this book is concerned with various issues regarding the impact of deafness on the development and education of deaf children, it seems appropriate to begin by identifying the population we are concerned with and by defining certain terms that sometimes cause confusion. The term *hearing impairment* is a generic term covering all degrees of hearing loss, regardless of when and how it was sustained. This heterogeneous group of individuals, however, can be subdivided further on the basis of a number of distinguishing features.

Traditionally, four descriptive variables have served to distinguish various subgroups within the general population possessing a hearing impairment, to which we would add a fifth. The four traditional variables are 1) degree of hearing impairment, 2) age at onset of hearing impairment, 3) type of hearing impairment, and 4) etiology of the hearing impairment. The fifth variable is the hearing status of the parents of deaf children. The first four variables are discussed in turn within this chapter, and discussion of the fifth variable occurs, where appropriate, in other chapters of the book.

DEGREE OF HEARING IMPAIRMENT

Although a number of audiometric techniques are available to the audiologist for assessing and evaluating the functioning and integrity of an individual's auditory mechanism, the degree of hearing impairment is typically described in terms of hearing threshold levels (HTL) for auditory pure tones. All sound can be described in terms of three physical parameters: 1) frequency, 2) intensity, and 3) time. Even complex speech sounds can eventually be reduced, physically, to various complex combinations of frequencies at different intensities lasting over periods of time. In auditory pure tone testing, an individual's threshold responses to sound elements are assessed along two of these physical dimensions: frequency and intensity.

An auditory threshold is defined as that point at which a particular sound element is barely heard 50% of the time, and in the case of auditory pure tone testing that means that point at which a particular frequency is just barely audible 50% of the time it is presented. Because more than one frequency is tested per ear, a threshold of intensity measured in decibels (dB) is obtained on each frequency tested. The decibel scale of intensity, as measured on the audiometer, ranges from – 10 dB to 110 dB and can be conceived of as a set of norms with 0 dB representing the statistically defined normal threshold (American National Standards Institute, 1969). It should be borne in mind that the decibel scale is a logarithmic scale and not a linear scale; thus, a sound stimulus that is at 20 dB is not twice as powerful as one that is at 10 dB, rather it is 10 times as powerful.

Although the human ear can perceive frequencies ranging from 20 Hz (low pitch) to 20,000 Hz (high pitch) tones, not all of the frequencies within this range are tested to establish the auditory threshold. Certain selected frequencies are sampled, particularly within what is considered the speech range. For example, the frequencies of 125, 250, 500, 1,000, 2,000, 4,000, and 8,000 Hz are typically tested. The speech range is the band of frequencies between 500 and 2,000 Hz. The importance of these speech frequencies is highlighted by the fact that often an individual's degree of hearing impairment is described in terms of a single number, i.e., a pure tone average (PTA), which is a summary statistic reflecting the average threshold response at 500, 1,000, and 2,000 Hz for any given ear. If only a single number is reported, usually it pertains to the more sensitive ear; otherwise two numbers are reported, one each for the right and left ears.

The audiogram itself is a pictorial representation of the dimensions tested and the subject's responses. Along the horizontal axis there are demarcations for the frequency values typically assessed, and along the vertical axis are demarcations for the decibel values from – 10 to 110, usually in 5-dB steps. The subject's individual threshold values as they are obtained are entered onto the intersection of the frequency by decibel grid for each ear. The line resulting from joining the series of such frequency by intensity points is the individual's audiogram.

Traditionally, certain audiometric classifications have been made based on degree of hearing impairment, as defined by the better ear pure tone average. These are: normal (− 10 dB to 27 dB), slight loss (27 dB to 40 dB), mild loss (41 dB to 55 dB), marked loss (56 dB to 70 dB), severe loss (71 dB to 90 dB), and profound loss 91 dB +). Individuals who have a hearing impairment no greater than a marked loss (less than 70 dB) are generally considered hard-of-hearing, whereas those who have a profound loss (greater than 90 dB) are considered deaf. The fourth category, severe loss, is a transition category between hard-of-hearing and deaf.

TYPE OF LOSS

The second defining variable refers to the type of impairment an individual has. There are four different types of hearing impairment, depending upon the site of lesion, or where along the auditory pathway the hearing loss is sustained. The four types are conductive, sensorineural, mixed, and central. A *conductive hearing impairment* refers to a disruption or blockage within all or part of the conductive mechanism of the outer or middle ear, and generally is medically remediable. When medical intervention is not possible, individuals having such an impairment often are excellent candidates for a hearing aid. *Sensorineural hearing impairments* are the result of damage to all or part of the inner ear, or cochlea, in which sensory or neural aspects of hearing begin. Damage to this portion of the hearing mechanism is irreversible, and individuals sustaining this type of impairment are only partially assisted by amplification. When an individual possesses both a sensorineural loss and a conductive loss, this condition is known as a *mixed loss. Central hearing impairments* may be the result of damage to the auditory neural network anywhere from the eighth auditory nerve, which transmits the sensory information from the inner ear to the cortex, up to and including the cortex itself.

AGE AT ONSET

The age at which a hearing impairment is sustained is the third traditional defining variable. A number of terms are used when discussing age at onset, and they use different reference points. Two important reference points are birth and the establishment of language (usually about 2 or 3 years of age and later). The term *congenital* refers to the fact that hearing impairment was sustained at birth, whereas the term *acquired* (or *adventitiously impaired*) refers to the fact that the hearing impairment was sustained some time after birth. The term *congenitally impaired* is often confused with the term *hereditary* and should not be. The former refers to a time frame, whereas the latter refers to an etiology. Similarly, the term *acquired impairment* is often confused with the notion of *postlingually* hearing impaired. To be *postlingually hearing impaired* is to have sustained a hearing impairment during or after the establishment of language, usually beginning around 2 or 3 years of age. To be classified as *prelingually hearing impaired* is to have sustained a hearing loss sometime prior to the establishment of language. The term *deafened* is but another name for an acquired or adventitiously sustained hearing impairment, although often it is particularly used to refer to those who have sustained an impairment postlingually.

ETIOLOGY

The final descriptive variable of importance for our purposes is etiology. Etiology is important because many of the causes of hearing impairments often result in one or more additional problems. As many as 25% of what we define as the deaf population have one or more additional complicating handicaps (Gentile and McCarthy, 1973). In general, the various etiologies can be subdivided into endogenous and exogenous types.

An *endogenous etiology* is the result of some biological cause or process, such as heredity, syndromes, metabolic and endocrine disorders, and blood incompatibilities (for example, Rh incompatibility). *Exogenous etiologies* are the result of some accident or of some foreign object or agent either blocking or destroying some aspect of the auditory mechanism. Included with the general category of exogenous etiologies are various accidents, obstructions, drugs, poisons, allergies, bacterial infections (e.g., meningitis), viral infections (e.g., mumps, rubella, and measles), and birth accidents (e.g., prematurity, birth injury, and anoxia). Many of these etiologies, such as viral infections, may operate to induce a hearing impairment postnatally (after birth) by affecting the individual directly, while others may operate indirectly by first affecting the mother and then the child prenatally, during pregnancy.

EDUCATIONAL DEFINITION OF DEAFNESS

For our purposes in this book, the deaf child or adult is one who sustained a profound (91 dB or greater), primarily sensorineural hearing impairment prelingually, caused by either exogenous or endogenous factors. Such individuals typically may only be aware of loud auditory stimuli and thus may not learn language auditorily or spontaneously. Complete description of a hearing impaired individual or population should include at least hearing threshold level, age at onset of hearing impairment, and type and etiology of the impairment. All of the variables important to description of hearing populations are, of course, similarly important with hearing impaired populations, such as IQ and socioeconomic status of family. *Much of the confusion in research and practice in the education of deaf children arises from incomplete descriptions of the populations under consideration and from generalization of findings to dissimilar populations.*

INCIDENCE ESTIMATES

Probably the earliest attempt to obtain any systematic data regarding the incidence of deafness in the United States was in the late 1700s when Francis Green conducted a survey in order to justify the establishment of a school for deaf children in America. At that time only 75 persons were definitely identified as being deaf in New England, although it was estimated that 500 such individuals existed in the country as a whole. Some years later another parent of a hearing impaired child, also in an attempt to establish a school for deaf children in the United States, conducted a similar survey of all school-age deaf children. In this survey, 80 deaf children were identified in New England and 800 deaf children were estimated in the country as a whole (Bender, 1960). From 1830 to 1930 the United States Bureau of the Census attempted to enumerate deaf persons in each decennial census, but the results obtained were highly variable. Because of the variable nature of the data, it was concluded that, given the methods used, no reliable census of hearing impaired persons could be made, and it was recommended that a separate agency be established to collect this information.

It was not until 1956 when funds were appropriated for the establishment of the National Health Survey that more reliable and systematic data were collected. As a part of the 1965 and 1971 Health Interview Surveys of adults, questions regarding hearing impairment were included, and in 1960 and 1963 selected samples of adults in the Health Examination Survey were given audiometric assessments of hearing. As a part of the latter survey, 7,119 noninstitutionalized children were also assessed, and the incidence of children having a slight loss or greater loss according to our definitions was 887/100,000. Similar results were obtained by the National Speech and Hearing survey of 1968–69. Both of these studies, however, excluded children in residential schools for deaf children. The most recent figures on the number of deaf children in various programs for deaf children are reported in the next section of this chapter.

EDUCATIONAL PROGRAMS

Table 1 shows the numbers of deaf students in various types of educational programs in 1979. It can be noted that males outnumber females by about 54% to 46%. It can also be seen that only about 30% of deaf students are

TABLE 1. Summary of schools and classes for deaf students in the United States – October, 1979[a]

Schools and classes	Program data				Student data						
	Number	Preschools	High schools	Programs for multiply handicapped students	Total enrollment	Males	Females	Residential students	Day students	Mainstreamed students	Partially mainstreamed students
Public residential schools	62	49	53	48	16,499	9,228	7,271	11,709	4,790	228	316
Private residential schools	6	6	2	2	579	313	266	424	155		3
Public day schools	53	46	30	25	6,908	3,617	3,291	459	6,449	732	1,787
Private day schools	16	13	117	3	534	269	265	10	524	91	30
Public day classes	337	237	3	170	17,481	9,147	8,334	27	17,454	5,529	7,042
Private day classes	19	15		5	294	147	147		294	22	103
Facilities for multiply handicapped students only	22	9	2		401	249	152	223	178		8
Facilities for students with specified handicaps	26	10		3	797	455	342	637	160	12	54
TOTALS	541	385	207	256	43,493	23,425	20,068	13,489	30,004	6,614	9,343

[a]Adapted from W. N. Craig and H. B. Craig (eds.), Directory of Services for the Deaf, American Annals of the Deaf, 1980, 125, p. 179.

residential students and about 70% are day students. This is a reversal of the situation that prevailed as recently as 20 years ago. Since about 1945 there has been a consistent trend for deaf students to be enrolled in day programs, and in the mid-1960s the majority enrollment shifted from residential to day. There has also been an increase in those deaf children identified as multiply handicapped, to where they now represent more than 20% of the total population.

In addition to a rapid increase in the number of deaf students enrolled in day programs, there also has been a large increase in deaf students attending postsecondary institutions. Schein and Bushnaq (1962) noted that in 1960 only about 1.78% of deaf students leaving lower schools were attending college-level institutions, as compared to 9.3% of the general population. Comparable data for the present time are not available, but a rough totalling of figures from various sources makes it likely that more than 50% of the deaf students leaving secondary level institutions are now attending postsecondary programs of some type.

More than 1,500 students attend Gallaudet College, a federally funded but privately incorporated college in Washington, D.C. The college was established for deaf students by an Act of Congress in 1864 with a charter signed by President Lincoln. The National Technical Institute for the Deaf, established by an Act of Congress in 1968 as an affiliate of the Rochester Institute of Technology in Rochester, New York, enrolls about 900 students. Three regional postsecondary programs were established in the 1960s with federal funding in St. Paul, Minnesota, Seattle, Washington, and New Orleans, Louisiana. A fourth such program at California State University at Northridge was funded in 1964. With funds from federal programs for the vocational training of handicapped students, many junior colleges throughout the country have established postsecondary programs for deaf students during the past decade. In addition to specially funded and staffed programs, many of the general institutions of higher education in the United States enroll qualified deaf students. Quigley, Jenne, and Phillips (1969) reported on several hundred such students, and Ogden (1979) reported extensively on an even larger group.

These data show that an extensive system of education exists for deaf students in the United States from preschool through college. Perhaps the only significant gap in the system exists in the period from birth to about 3 or 4 years of age. Although these are not usually considered school years, they are perhaps the most important years for the development of language and communication, and development in those areas is vital and extremely difficult for deaf children. The importance of the infant and early childhood years has been recognized since the recorded beginnings of the education of deaf children in the late 16th and early 17th centuries (Bonet, 1620), but systematic programs in the United States probably began only with the establishment of the John Tracy Clinic in Los Angeles in 1943. This private clinic's program was founded on the principle that development of language and communication had to be fostered in deaf children in infancy and early childhood in much the same manner as in hearing children. In this process the parents must play a major role.

The program of the John Tracy Clinic has provided the model for many other parent-infant and early childhood education programs for deaf children that have been established throughout the country. These programs, however, have usually been established on an individual basis rather than as a general service of the public school system. They need to be made available to all deaf children and their parents as a regular service of the public schools.

2

LANGUAGE AND COMMUNICATION METHODS

The primary issue in the education of deaf children is the form of language and communication that should be used by and with the children in school and in their infant and early childhood years in the home. In this chapter we 1) present the issue, 2) define and trace historically the major communication methods used today, 3) present and discuss the research on the issue, and 4) try to reach some tentative conclusions about this vital concern.

LANGUAGE DEVELOPMENT

Language has been defined as "a code whereby ideas about the world are represented through a conventional system of signals for communication" (Bloom and Lahey, 1978, p. 4). All known human societies have developed signal systems for communication based on the spoken word, using the aural-oral channel for reception and expression. Most members of societies acquire the spoken language of their group in an apparently effortless fashion during the first few years of life. Many of the details of this acquisition are known from linguistic and psycholinguistic research and can be found in a number of basic texts (Dale, 1976; de Villiers and de Villiers, 1978). Only a few general points are of concern here. If an infant has a reasonably intact sensory system, has no severe intellectual or cognitive deficit, is exposed to a reasonably stimulating environment, and has reasonably verbal parents or parent surrogates who provide a reasonably warm and loving atmosphere and communicate reasonably fluently with the infant, an auditory-based language system will be internalized effortlessly by the child. This internalized, auditory-based language system will serve as a foundation of the child's receptive and expressive language in early childhood and as the base on which reading and writing and all education factors related to them will later be developed.

The word "reasonably" is used deliberately. Early language development seems to be surprisingly resistant to disruption by either organismic or environmental factors and, apparently, substantial deficiencies can be tolerated in the sensory system, in the cognitive realm, in environmental stimulation, and in parent-child relationships without language development becoming either seriously disordered or delayed. However, severe and prolonged deprivation in any of these areas will eventually produce communication and language problems, with the severity of disorder being at least roughly related to the severity of deprivation. The primary problem seems to be interference with the establishment of easy and fluent communication between the child and the immediate figures in his environment (usually the parents, and particularly the mother). Because this easy and fluent communication in humans depends upon a reasonably intact auditory system, deafness will certainly produce a massive disruption of the normal development of language and communication. Parental and educational practices with deaf individuals from infancy to early adulthood, therefore, should have as their primary goal the establishment of an easy and fluent system of communication that can be internalized as a language foundation on which the secondary language systems of reading and writing can then be developed.

There would probably be little disagreement with this statement by any who work with deaf children and youth. The disagreements arise in just what *type of language* should be established and by what *communication means* it should be established. It is commonly accepted that there is just a single issue here: the form of communication to be used. Actually, there are two issues: the form of communication to be used and the language to be used. There are two distinct communication forms (oral and manual) and two distinct languages (American Sign Language and English) that can be used in various combinations. Before proceeding to a discussion of the communication and language issues and the research relating to them, we define the best-known language intervention systems that are presently used with at least some portion of the population of deaf children and youth. [The definitions given here appear also in Quigley and King (in press).] There is not complete agreement in the field on definitions of these terms, and a recommended source for other definitions is Caccamise and Drury (1976).

LANGUAGE INTERVENTION SYSTEMS

The language intervention systems can be classified into three general categories: American Sign Language, Manual English, and Oral English. Within each of these categories are variations, depending upon the form of communication used and its approximation to American Sign Language or English. Other types of classifications exist. The one used here is not being presented as superior to others, but fits best the authors' educational organization of the chapter material.

American Sign Language   American Sign Language is manual communication in the form of signs used as a language. It is important to remember that this is not only a different form of communication from oral communication, but also a different language from English and other languages. Concepts are conveyed in signs and other *gestural* movements (manual communication) and in a grammar different from English or other spoken languages. Although some researchers question whether American Sign Language (ASL) is a bona fide language or a secondary signal system (Schlesinger and Namir, 1978), many language researchers present evidence for its status as a language (Stokoe, 1960; Friedman, 1977; Siple, 1978; Klima and Bellugi, 1979). ASL meets the definition of language as expressed earlier, and it has functioned as a primary vehicle of communication among deaf people for centuries. Whether it has developed to the point where it can perform all of the educational functions of spoken languages is perhaps still open to question and research. In general, then, ASL differs from oral English communication not only in its form (signs), but also in its composition and status as a language.

Manual English   Manual English is a term applied to a variety of systems that use signs, fingerspelling, or gestures separately or in combinations to represent English manually. Some of the best known are described here, with the closest approximation to English syntax (fingerspelling) listed first and the others listed in decreasing approximation to English syntax.

Fingerspelling   The manual alphabet, or fingerspelling, has 26 handshapes representing the 26 letters of the written English alphabet. These handshapes can be used to spell English words manually, just as the written alphabet can be used to write them. This allows an exact representation of written English to be used as a means of communication by and with deaf people (Quigley, 1969).

Cued Speech   The Cued Speech system might also be classified as a form of Oral English, but because it uses manual cues to supplement spoken English, we have chosen to classify it as a form of Manual English. In this system, eight handshapes are used to represent phonetic elements of speech that are not readily visible for *speechreading*, which is another term roughly synonymous with *lipreading*. These handcues are designed to supplement the spoken message so that the combination of speech and handcues provides a visibly intelligible message to the deaf person. The system was deliberately constructed in such a manner that it could *not* function alone as a manual system of communication (Cornett, 1967).

Linguistics of Visual English (LOVE)   The signs of the Linguistics of Visual English system are supposed to parallel speech rhythm; that is, a three-syllable word would be represented by a three-movement sign. LOVE signs resemble ASL signs much less than do the signs in the other systems of Manual English. The system was designed for preschool and kindergarten deaf children, but is not widely used (Wampler, 1972).

Seeing Essential English (SEE-I)   The Seeing Essential English system was designed to use ASL signs plus signs invented to represent both root words and the inflectional system of English, so that a close manual approximation of English could be realized. The system functionally classifies English words into three groups: 1) basic words, 2) compound words, and 3) complex words. The basic words consist of whole-word forms or root words. Because there is not a one-to-one correspondence between ASL signs and English words, three criteria were established to guide the use of a sign for a particular word: meaning, spelling, and sound. A single sign is used when any two of the three criteria are the same for two or more English words. For example, the English word "light" has several common meanings in English — an entity in itself, not dark, and weight. However, because the spelling and sound are the same in English, SEE-I uses a single sign to represent them. (ASL, alternatively, has separate signs for each of these meanings.) Compound words are formed by using the basic sign for each of the component words. This is done if the component words in the compound words retain enough of their original meaning to make them consistent with the meaning of the compound words as a whole. If, however, the consistency between the component parts and the whole is lost, a new sign is developed. Complex words are formed by the addition of one or more *affixes* (inflections) to a root word. SEE-I has more than 118 different affixes representing a large variety of both regular and irregular inflectional forms (Anthony, 1966).

Signing Exact English (SEE-II)   SEE-II, like SEE-I, classifies English words into three groups: 1) basic, 2) compound, and 3) complex, and the basic words are treated as in SEE-I, with the same two-out-of-three criteria rule. The major difference between SEE-I and SEE-II is the determination of what constitutes a basic or root word, and thus the manner in which compound and complex words are formed. SEE-I creates a number of complex words, such as "general" and "interview" by affixing inflections to root words, such as "gen" and "view," respectively, whereas SEE-II treats these as being basic words. The manner in which compound and complex words are formed is similar to SEE-I, even though the foundation of basic words differs. The SEE-II system only employs approximately 70 affixes and is composed of 61% ASL signs, 18% modified ASL signs, and 21% newly invented signs (Gustason, Pfetzing, and Zawolkow, 1975).

Signed English   The Signed English system was devised as a semantic representation of English for children between the ages of 1 and 6 years. ASL signs are used in English word order with 14 sign markers being added to represent a portion of the inflectional system of English. The lexical use of signs in this system probably is closer to the ASL use of signs than any of the preceding systems (Bornstein, 1973).

Ameslish, Siglish   Ameslish and Siglish are terms for the system of communication often used by deaf people when they wish to use manual communication to represent English rather than American Sign Language. ASL signs and fingerspelling (for English words that have no sign equivalents) are used in English word order without use of the English inflectional system. Some aspects of ASL grammar, including sign space, pluralization, and directionality, are used at times. This system is also referred to as Pidgin Sign English (Bragg, 1973).

Oral English   As the term implies, Oral English is the use of English in oral form as used among hearing people. The two major forms of this approach used with deaf children are the *Aural/Oral Method* and the *Acoupedic (or Unisensory) Method*. The *Aural/Oral Method* employs speech and speechreading by and with the deaf child and places great emphasis on the early and consistent use of high-quality amplification and auditory training. In the *Acoupedic Method* speechreading is minimized and major emphasis is placed on amplification and auditory training to develop as fully as possible any residual hearing the deaf child might have.

Various combinations of these language intervention systems or communication systems have been utilized as established teaching methods in the education of deaf children. The use of only oral means of communication is known as the *Oral Method*. The combined use of fingerspelling and oral methods is known as the *Rochester Method*. The combined use of manual communication (signs and fingerspelling) and oral methods used in English word order is known as the *Simultaneous Method*. The other term in common usage currently is *Total Communication*. This is a system that advocates the use of any means of communication by and with the deaf child that seems to be useful. It could include any or all of the systems that have been presented here.

HISTORICAL ANTECEDENTS

It is often believed that some of these methods or communication systems are recent developments in the education of deaf children and youth. In actuality, each approach presently in use was developed, at least in some precursor form, 50 years or more ago. What seem to be recent developments are mostly improvements in technology, refinements of methods, or merely changes in names.

The Oral Method, which uses speech and speechreading as the primary means of communicating with and by deaf students, has its roots in the work of Pablo Ponce de León (the first recorded teacher of deaf children) in Spain in the 16th century, of Samuel Heinicke, the founder of the German Method in the 18th century, and of the Clarke School for the Deaf in the United States in the 19th century. The Neo-oralism (fingerspelling and speech) of the Soviet Union in the 1950s is directly related to the Rochester Method used in the Rochester School for the Deaf in the United States since 1878, which in turn is directly related to the methods of Juan Bonet, who advocated the use of a one-handed manual alphabet in conjunction with speech in his book published in 1620. American Sign Language (ASL), which is utilized widely among deaf people at the present time, was directly influenced by the French language of signs brought to the United States by Thomas Hopkins Gallaudet and Laurent Clerc[1] in 1817. The use of the native language system of the deaf society (in this case, French Sign Language) was initially attempted by the Abbé Charles Michel de l'Épée in the 18th century, who also developed a system of methodical signs. These methodical signs, which were expanded by Abbé Roche Ambroise Sicard and were used to adapt the French language of signs to conform to the grammar or structure of spoken French, are a direct precursor of Seeing Essential English (SEE-I) and Signing Exact English (SEE-II), which use natural signs and invented signs to make ASL conform to the structure of English. It is interesting to note that Sicard's expansion resulted in making the language of signs slower and more cumbersome, and gradually the original language of signs reasserted itself (Moores, 1978). The Acoupedic (or Unisensory Method), which emphasizes the use of audition and de-emphasizes the use of vision in early education of deaf children, is a direct descendant of the methods of Dr. Max Goldstein in the United States and of Urbantschitz in Austria during the early part of the 20th century. The Simultaneous Method, which uses speech and manual communication (signs and fingerspelling), has been in use since the time of Gallaudet in the United States and of Sicard in France in the

---

[1]Laurent Clerc was the first deaf teacher of deaf individuals in the United States. Thomas Hopkins Gallaudet brought Clerc to the United States from France, after Gallaudet completed his studies with Abbé Roche Ambroise Sicard, to help establish the first school for deaf children in the United States.

18th century. Total Communication, in the judgment of the authors and of many others, is essentially another name for the Simultaneous Method.

As can be seen, then, these supposedly modern communication methods and systems actually have a rich and varied historical heritage. For more detailed historical accounts of the education of deaf people, the reader is referred to Bender (1960), Davis and Silverman (1978), and Moores (1978).

Most methods today use amplification, auditory training, reading, writing, and a variety of audiovisual devices and techniques. These do not serve to differentiate the methods. What seems to differentiate them is whether they use oral only, manual only, or some combination of these, and also which form of manual communication is used. From the time of de l'Épée and Heinicke, controversy has existed about the relative merits of various communication methods for educating deaf students. During that period of more than 200 years, arguments have been pressed by proponents of the various approaches with evangelical zeal and little research evidence. Unfortunately, this is still largely the case today, but during the past 20 years an increasing amount of research has been undertaken on the matter. Currently we have at least one or two studies on most of the approaches, which permits some reasoned consideration of the problem. Now that the problem has been presented, various communication approaches defined, and historical antecedents briefly traced, we present some representative studies that have been conducted on the merits of the various approaches.

Studies of various communication methods and of educational and other effects of those methods are presented in three categories: American Sign Language (ASL), Manual English, and Oral English. The investigations can also be classified as direct or indirect studies of the problem. For example, studies comparing deaf children of deaf parents to deaf children of hearing parents are indirect studies of the effects of early manual communication. The fact that deaf children of deaf parents score higher than matched deaf children of hearing parents on certain variables does not mean that manual communication is the causative factor. That is *inferred* from the studies, but this might be a somewhat shaky inference, as we will show. Direct studies comparing the effectiveness of various methodologies are much rarer than the indirect studies, perhaps because they are much more difficult to design, conduct, and interpret. We present both indirect and direct studies within each of the three categories whenever possible.

AMERICAN SIGN LANGUAGE

Although the majority of adult deaf Americans probably use American Sign Language in some form, only a small percentage learn it from their parents in early childhood in the manner in which hearing children acquire spoken English. Most deaf individuals learn American Sign Language by interacting with deaf peers who learned it from deaf parents, or in some similar indirect fashion. Deaf children of deaf parents form a special grouping within the general population of deaf children, and, because several studies using groups of them are discussed here, certain basic facts should be understood. First, only about 3% of deaf children have two deaf parents, with an additional 6% having at least one deaf parent (Rawlings and Jensema, 1977). Second, not all deaf children of deaf parents are exposed to ASL in infancy and early childhood, as is commonly supposed. As we indicate, some deaf parents use Manual English with their deaf children for a specific purpose (the early development of English), and still others use oral communication with their deaf children.

One of the most notable recent developments in research on language and communication with deaf children has been the great influx of linguists and psycholinguists into research on the nature and acquisition of American Sign Language. Although many individuals working with deaf people as well as deaf people themselves have long regarded ASL as a genuine language, examination of the nature and structure of ASL began with publication in 1960 of a monograph titled *Sign Language Structure: An Outline of the Visual Communication Systems of the American Deaf* (Stokoe, 1960). This pioneering work describes a linguistic analysis of ASL that supports the concept that ASL has a cheremic structure analogous to the phonetic and morphemic structure of spoken languages. That is, it was discovered that individual signs, like individual spoken words, were comprised of smaller units (such as handshape configurations, place of articulation, and movement), which, in and of themselves, were meaningless; that these cheremes, or manual communication phoneme equivalents, formed signs under a system of definable rules; and that signs were combined into a connected and fluent language by a system of grammatical rules—a syntax—thus completing the analogy of ASL with spoken languages. This linguistic approach has been followed in a number of studies and books on psycholinguistic analysis of the acquisition of ASL, some of which provide detailed information on stages in ASL acquisition by deaf children of ASL-using deaf parents (Friedman, 1977; Siple, 1978; Klima and Bellugi, 1979; Wilbur, 1979). A sympathetic and generally readable treatment of ASL, including its linguistic, psycholinguistic, sociolinguistic, and neurolinguistic aspects, can be found in Lane and Grosjean (1980). This is a good introduction, for specialists and nonspecialists, to the general nature and history of ASL and to the myths and difficulties that have surrounded its use.

The linguistic research conducted to date indicates that ASL has the essential characteristics of a language as do spoken languages, and that it can function as a fluent system of communication with and among deaf people. Simple observation indicates the same things. Psycholinguistic research indicates that the acquisition of ASL follows stages similar to those of spoken language acquisition and that the acquisition of language in a visual-manual modality parallels the acquisition of language in the oral-aural modality. From this it has been argued that ASL is the "natural" language of American deaf children and that it should be developed in them in infancy and early childhood as their first language, with English later being taught as a second language, or that both ASL and English should be used concurrently in a bilingual situation.

Some studies have been undertaken that note the effects of early exposure to ASL on later educational development, including the development of English. Although it is possible to design rigorous experimental studies of the issue, the conduct of such actual studies is not possible because of social and practical restrictions. Consequently, investigations of the problem are mostly *in situ* studies (studies that take advantage of certain naturally occurring situations among subgroups of the general populations of deaf children). In this case, most of the research involves studies of deaf children of deaf parents. It is reasonable to assume that many (but not all) such children will be raised in an environment where ASL is the dominant form of language and communication used by the parents and the children.

The earliest published studies using the paradigm of comparing deaf children of deaf parents to deaf children of hearing parents revealed that the former group of children had significantly higher performance than the latter group on measures of educational achievement, reading, vocabulary, written language, speechreading, fingerspelling, the language of signs, and psychosocial development (Quigley and Frisina, 1961; Stuckless and Birch, 1966; Meadow, 1967). These early studies were somewhat equivocal, however, regarding the relative comparability of these two groups in terms of speech intelligibility. It should be noted, too, that the differences found in the studies were differences in group *averages*. Many of the *individual* deaf children of hearing parents outperformed many of the *individual* deaf children of deaf parents, indicating that other factors in addition to hearing status of parents were involved in the performances of the subjects.

Although there seems to be little doubt that, on the average, deaf children of deaf parents perform at a higher level on certain important educational variables than do children from the general population of deaf children of hearing parents, there is some disagreement as to how these findings should be interpreted. The common assumption has been that the differences were the product of early exposure to manual communication, most likely in the form of ASL, and that therefore this form of communication should be used generally with deaf children. Other factors have been proposed, however, as possible causative agents in the process. First, the fact that deaf children of deaf parents are genetically deaf makes them much less prone to the multiple involvements that can result from deafness produced by etiologies like maternal rubella during pregnancy. This absence of complicating factors might have given deaf children of deaf parents an educational and communicative advantage. Second, the differences in favor of deaf children of deaf parents could be the result of the fact that such parents are less traumatized by the birth of a deaf child and are more likely than hearing parents to provide the type of healthy emotional and learning environment that could aid in the early development of language and communication. Third, the comparison groups of deaf children of hearing parents in all of the studies had not had early and intensive exposure to language solely through oral communication, which would be the oral equivalent of the early and intensive exposure the deaf children of deaf parents probably had through manual communication. Several studies have addressed these criticisms.

Partial evidence de-emphasizing the impact and importance of genetic factors comes from a study designed to control for such factors (Vernon and Koh, 1970). In this study, two matched groups of genetically deaf students, one group having deaf parents and the other having genetic deafness but hearing parents, were compared. If the genetic factor were responsible for the differences commonly found in favor of deaf children of deaf parents, then the two groups in this study should have performed equally, because all children in both groups had genetic deafness. However, this was not the case. The group with deaf parents outperformed the group with hearing parents on various educational and communication variables.

The factor of parental acceptance of the deaf child has also been investigated. In one study a comparison was made among three groups of deaf students: a group of deaf children with deaf parents who used only oral communication with their deaf children, a group of deaf children with deaf parents who used manual communication, and a group of deaf children with hearing parents (Corson, 1973). In general, it was found that both groups with deaf parents outperformed the group with hearing parents, but that the group with oral deaf parents performed as well or better than the group with manual deaf parents on tests of reading, social adjustment, self-image, speech intelligibility, speech reading, and other variables. This would indicate that parental acceptance of, and attitude toward, the deaf child might be as important as the type of communication used in the home.

Finally, a third study has been performed to explore the factor of intensive early exposure to oral communication (Brasel and Quigley, 1977). This study was designed to investigate the effects of type and intensity of communication and type of language input in early life on the later development of language and communication ability in deaf students. Four groups of deaf children were studied. One group had deaf parents who had used Manual English (Siglish, Ameslish, Pidgin Sign English) with their deaf children in infancy and early childhood, a second group had deaf parents who used ASL with their deaf children, a third group had hearing parents who obtained intensive oral education for their deaf children in infancy and early childhood, and a fourth group had hearing parents who left the education of their children to the general school system. Various comparisons among these groups permitted investigation of the effects of type of communication (oral and manual), type of language (ASL and English), and intensity of early language and communication input (early intensive oral and early intensive manual). It was possible, therefore, to study the effects of early intensive use of American Sign Language, Manual English, and Oral English. The results showed that the Manual English group was significantly superior to the other groups on almost all of the language and communication variables studied. The group with early exposure to ASL and the group with early intensive oral education performed about equally on most variables. The group with the average oral education was significantly below the other three groups on most variables. It was concluded that manual communication provided advantages over oral communication in early language development and that Manual English provided advantages over ASL.

These studies, then, suggest that the superior performance of deaf children of deaf parents might not be exclusively because of the use of the language of signs, nor because the children are genetically hearing impaired and therefore "free" of complicating multiple handicaps. Other factors, such as the parental attitudes toward the child and the type of manual communication, might also play significant roles.

MANUAL ENGLISH

The studies discussed here follow the order of definitions of the various forms of Manual English presented earlier. It should be remembered in evaluating all studies using manual communication that the forms rarely exist in their pure state. Frequent borrowings take place, and it is often difficult to determine whether or not a method was utilized as precisely as was expected in any study.

The use of fingerspelling, which had its origins in the work of Bonet more than 350 years ago, underwent a resurgence in the 1950s and 1960s, following publication of studies in the Soviet Union that indicated that its early use with deaf children produced significantly improved vocabulary development (Morkovin, 1960). The Soviet investigators claimed that use of the method succeeded in developing vocabularies of more than 2,000 words in deaf children between the ages of 2 and 6 years, an age period during which most deaf children in the United States might have vocabularies of only a few dozen words. The investigators claimed also that fingerspelling facilitated the development of speech and speechreading.

In the United States, two studies of this method were conducted between 1963 and 1968 (Quigley, 1969). One study was a longitudinal survey of the use of the Rochester Method (fingerspelling and speech) in five residential schools, and the other was an experimental comparison of the Rochester Method and the Oral Method with preschool-aged deaf children in two residential schools. In both studies, the children exposed to the Rochester Method outperformed their comparison groups on most measures of language, communication, and educational achievement. This was particularly true in the experimental study with preschool-aged deaf children, in which the children exposed to the Rochester Method outperformed the children exposed to the Oral Method.

Cued Speech has been heavily promoted but little investigated in the United States or elsewhere. This system is similar to the phonetic alphabet systems in use in Denmark and in other European countries during the 19th century, in which handcues are used to represent the phonetic elements of speech not easily visible for speechreading. Supposedly, the addition of these handcues provides a complete and visually intelligible message for the deaf child.

No studies have been conducted comparing this teaching method to other teaching methods. There have been, however, two studies conducted to assess the progress of a group of deaf children in the receptive use of Cued Speech after one and then two years of exposure to the systems (Ling and Clarke, 1975; Clarke and Ling, 1976). Although the children's initial speech reception scores were better under the condition of lipreading plus cues, as opposed to lipreading alone, their overall performance was poor. Upon retesting a year later, the children made substantial gains in the receptive use of the Cued Speech system, with the maintenance of a lipreading plus cues superiority. Complete mastery was still not noted. The addition of an auditory component did not increase performance significantly.

A master's thesis has also been completed (Nicholls, 1979) investigating the use of Cued Speech in a school in Australia. Like the previous studies, the thesis compared the speech reception scores obtained under different conditions involving various combinations of audition, lipreading, and cueing of profoundly deaf children exposed to the system for a minimum of 4 years. It was noted that the children developed a high degree of proficiency in the system and that the children performed best in conditions employing lipreading plus cues and audition. Although a high degree of receptive Cued Speech ability was noted, speech and language were not similarly improved.

The language acquisition of three deaf children who had been exposed from an early age (15 months to 3 years) to Seeing Essential English (SEE-I) has been described (Schlesinger and Meadow, 1972). By comparing the results with reported acquisition stages and rates of development of spoken language by hearing children, the investigators concluded that the deaf children were acquiring grammatical competence in the same sequence as hearing children but at a somewhat slower rate. Their overall development in syntax and vocabulary were still considered rapid, however.

Signing Exact English (SEE-II) is apparently the system most widely used with deaf children at present (Jordan, Gustason, and Rosen, 1976). The effects of SEE-II on the language development of deaf students has been studied (Babb, 1979). In this study, one group of deaf students had been exposed to SEE-II only in school from about 3 years of age, whereas the other group had been exposed to this method in both school and the home from about the same age. Both groups had more than 10 years of exposure to the system when they were compared on the *Test of Syntactic Abilities*, the *Stanford Achievement Test*, and a test of written language ability. The two groups of deaf students were compared to each other, to a hearing comparison group, to groups of children from a previous study (Brasel and Quigley, 1977), and to normative data for hearing impaired students on the *Stanford Achievement Test* (Office of Demographic Studies, 1972).

The deaf group that was exposed to SEE-II in both home and school performed almost as well as the Manual English (Ameslish, Siglish, Pidgin Sign) group in the previously cited study by Brasel and Quigley, which was the highest performing group in that study. The group that was exposed to SEE-II only in school had much lower scores on all tests than these two groups, and performed no better than the Average Oral group from the Brasel and Quigley study and no better than the norms for the general population of deaf students on the *Stanford Achievement Test*.

Bornstein, Saulnier, and Hamilton (1980) conducted a 4-year study to evaluate the effects of Signed English. Subjects of the study were 20 4-year-old prelingually deaf children with a mean hearing loss of 88 dB. The children were instructed in speech and Signed English by their teachers. Parents also made attempts to communicate simultaneously in Signed English and speech with the children. Children were evaluated each year for 4 years using the *Peabody Picture Vocabulary Test*, the *Northwestern Syntax Screening Test*, and a morphology test designed to measure skill with the inflections used in Signed English.

Results were that, at the end of 4 years, the vocabulary level of the children was similar to the vocabulary of hearing impaired children 3 years older. Their rate of growth of receptive vocabulary was roughly 43% of that observed in hearing children. The growth of their skill in reception of syntactic markers was similar to that of hearing children, and the subjects did not stop using their voices as a result of using simultaneous communication.

Moores (1978) conducted a longitudinal study comparing various types of preschool programs. Seven types of early intervention programs were examined with a research model designed to determine the preferred approach for a particular child at a particular stage of development. Moores' description of the research is as follows:

> The programs were selected to represent a number of important components of various early intervention systems. The programs differed as to methodology (auditory, oral-aural, Rochester Method, total communication); setting (day, residential); orientation (traditional nursery, academic, cognitive); emphasis (parent-centered, child-centered); and placement (integrated, self-contained). Each participating program was considered a strong representative of a particular intervention mode.

Major differences were found among the programs, primarily on receptive communication ability, with the programs using Total Communication and the Rochester Method outperforming the other groups. The highest combined average receptive communication score on printed word; sound alone; sound and speechreading; sound, speechreading and fingerspelling; and sound, speechreading, and signs was obtained by the subjects in the program that started with the Rochester Method and later tracked children into either Total Communication (Simultaneous Method) or oral-aural classes.

ORAL ENGLISH

Although the studies cited in the sections on American Sign Language and Manual English included investigations containing groups of children exposed to oral-aural methods of instruction, supporters of oral programs would contend that those oral groups did not represent the best possible oral approaches. There is considerable justification for that contention. It is likely that actively pursued and comprehensive oral programs exist only in three major schools in the United States: Central Institute for the Deaf in St. Louis, Missouri; Clarke School for the Deaf in Northampton, Massachusetts; and St. Joseph's Institute for the Deaf in St. Louis, Missouri. There are only a few other such programs. As long as comparative studies fail to include groups of subjects from one or more of these schools, results of the studies must be viewed with some reservation. It is still defensible to infer from the comparative studies that have been done, however, that children exposed to certain forms of combined oral and manual communication outperform children who have been exposed to *typical oral programs* on certain important language and educational variables. It is possible that the oral programs as exemplified by the schools just named require conditions that cannot be met in the public schools. This is discussed further in the concluding section of this chapter. Studies cited in the present section on Oral English are mostly studies involving children from incontestably oral programs.

In one study of the oral language ability of young deaf children, deaf and hearing children between 5 and 13 years of age were administered the *Northwestern Syntax Screening Test (NSST)*, and spontaneous language samples were obtained from the same children (Pressnell, 1973). It was found that syntactic ability developed much more slowly in the deaf children than in their hearing peers. Older deaf children performed better than younger ones on the *NSST*, with a spurt in language development occurring between 5 and 9 years of age. No significant improvement with age was found for the deaf children on their spontaneous language samples.

It has been argued that oral deaf children with good language skills are integrated into regular classrooms with hearing children and thus are usually not included in studies of language performance of oral deaf children in special schools and classes. In seeking to confirm this, one group of investigators (Geers and Moog, 1978) tested and retested 14 oral deaf children, some of whom had been integrated into regular classrooms. Children were tested with the *Developmental Sentence Analysis* (Lee, 1974) and with the *Carrow Elicited Language Inventory* (Carrow, 1974). This study supported the finding of a spurt in language growth for the oral deaf children who were between the ages of 4 and 9 years. It also revealed that the oral deaf children, who were between the ages of 4 and 9 years, generally had language scores below those for 3-year-old hearing children. As expected, the deaf children who had been integrated into regular classrooms were found to have significantly higher spontaneous language scores than the children who remained in the Central Institute for the Deaf. The children who remained in special classes, however, did better on imitated language.

Another group of investigators (Doehring, Bonnycastle, and Ling, 1978) also conducted a study to assess the reading and language skills of a group of hearing impaired children enrolled in regular classrooms. In this study the 10 (of 21) subjects who were classified as profoundly hearing impaired (91+ dB) scored at or above normal grade level on 9 of 11 reading-related tests, but all subjects were below normal grade level on at least 4 of 5 language measures. It is surprising to note that the profoundly hearing impaired subjects outperformed the severely impaired subjects, a finding that the investigators attributed to the earlier identification and training of profoundly hearing impaired children.

In other studies it has been reported that, at the Clarke School for the Deaf, deaf students 8 to 10 years old had average reading scores on the *Stanford Achievement Test* at the second-to third-grade level, and students 17 to 18 years old scored on the average at the sixth-grade level (Magner, 1964). Former pupils of Central Institute for the Deaf (CID) increased their reading levels by 2.5 grades as compared to the national data of 0.8 grades reported by Furth (1966b) for the same age range — 10 to 16 years (Lane and Baker, 1974). This latter finding has been confirmed in another study using 52 students from the same school (CID) (Geers and Moog, 1978). Average reading scores rose from second-grade level for students 7 to 9 years old to almost fifth-grade level for students 13 to 15 years old. Because the students in CID tend to have higher IQs than the average for deaf students and come from families with high socioeconomic status (Ogden, 1979), it is difficult to relate these findings to those of previously cited studies.

The studies cited in this section indicate that deaf children in incontestably oral programs tend to develop better language skills than do deaf children in the general school population. It should be borne in mind that deaf children in these programs often are more select in socioeconomic status, IQ, and other factors than deaf children in general. Even given the select nature of the population, however, it has been claimed that a high degree of success in language development and in later occupational attainment can be obtained by students educated in aggressively Oral English programs.

This was confirmed in a study in which extensive information on 637 former students of the Central Institute for the Deaf, the Clarke School for the Deaf, and St. Joseph's Institute for the Deaf was reported (Ogden, 1979). The respondents were found to be highly successful in terms of their academic and occupational accomplishments. A majority of the 441 respondents who were out of school at the time of the study were engaged in professional level occupations, and 30.6% of them had completed at least a 4-year undergraduate college education, which is much higher than the national averages of 19.6% and 11.6% of white men and women with a similar level of education. The figure is even more impressive when it is considered that 39.2% of the 196 subjects still in school at the time of the survey were in institutions of higher education.

Quigley and King (in press) summarized the study in this manner:

> The subjects attributed their academic and occupational success in large measure to their development of Oral English. The great majority felt that their speech was readily understood by others and that they could understand speech well through speechreading. They believed their communication and language skills had enabled them to participate successfully in the general society. It should be noted, however, that the subjects came from academically and occupationally elite families. More than 43% of the fathers and 30% of the mothers completed a four-year college education. Of the fathers, 52.5% went on to studies ranging from graduate to postdoctoral, while 39.5% of the mothers did graduate to postdoctoral work. But, as stated earlier, in spite of the elite nature of the students involved, their success in acquiring Oral English and the contributions of that skill to their later success in life are impressive.

DISCUSSION

Several tentative conclusions can be drawn from the studies presented. It should be borne in mind that until many more studies have been conducted and much more evidence has been accumulated, conclusions can be only tentative, and, in some cases, can only be acts of faith. Some conclusions are in order, nonetheless, because the teacher, the clinician, and most importantly the parents, all must choose some communication and language system for communicating with and instructing the deaf child.

1. *The issue is both a communication and a language issue.* There are two main forms of communication (oral and manual) and two languages (ASL and English) involved in the issue. Lack of recognition of this dual nature of the issue sometimes leads to confusion in discussion and in definitions of methods. Various combinations of the form of communication and form of language have been defined in this chapter and categorized under the headings of American Sign Language (ASL), Manual English, and Oral English.

2. *The issue is social and cultural as well as a language and communication one.* Most of the marriages of deaf people in the United States are to other deaf people or to hard-of-hearing people, and a majority of deaf people pursue most of their social activities with other hearing impaired people (Schein and Delk, 1974) and with hearing people who can communicate in ASL or Manual English. The key factor is the language and communication. Because most deaf adults apparently use ASL as their language of choice, regardless of how they were educated, it is difficult to find any justification for placing restrictions on its use or on its natural evolution as a language. Difficulties arise, however, in deciding how ASL can be encouraged to flourish among children who know it and wish to use it, while at the same time developing in deaf children the dominant language of the society in which they must function, at least economically.

3. *Reasoning from questionable analogies currently complicates the issue.* It is frequently stated that deaf people form a minority culture in American society similar to black, Hispanic, and other minority groupings, and that therefore the dynamics, problems, and solutions of such minority cultures apply to deaf people. It is further reasoned from the cultural minority analogy that ASL is the "natural" language of deaf people in the United States, that it should be the original language developed with all deaf children, and that English should be taught as a second language or developed concurrently in a bilingual situation. The analogy is questionable on two counts. First, although black children are usually born to black parents, Spanish children to Spanish parents, and so forth, deaf children are usually born to *hearing* parents. Deaf children of deaf parents, for whom the analogy might be appropriate, form only a small minority of the population of deaf children — a minority within a minority. As noted earlier, only about 9% of deaf children have at least

one hearing impaired parent, with about one-third of those having two such parents. Thus, deaf children are not usually raised in families of deaf parents and siblings, but in families of hearing people. This leaves the cultural minority analogy and the conclusions derived from it open to question. The second questionable factor in this analogy is the designation of ASL as the "natural" language of American deaf people. This is considered in relation to the fourth tentative conclusion.

4. *Lack of agreed-upon uses of various terms currently confuses the issue.* An example of this confusion is the use of the term *natural language* to describe the use of ASL with deaf children. It seems reasonable to assume that the natural language for any child is the language with which the child is raised in infancy and early childhood and that becomes the fluent internalized language system on which later educational development is based. For deaf children of deaf parents this language is very likely to be ASL. As has been indicated (Corson, 1973; Brasel and Quigley, 1977), however, this is not always true even for deaf children of deaf parents. Of course, ASL is rarely the language of deaf children of hearing parents, who represent more than 90% of the population of deaf children. One answer to that is that it *should be* the case for those children also. Because deaf children of deaf parents on the average outperform deaf children of hearing parents, on a variety of important variables, then ASL should be the initial language of all deaf people. This is discussed further in the fifth conclusion. First, another term deserves consideration — Total Communication.

Total Communication (as defined by Denton, 1970) is "the right of a deaf child to learn to use all forms of communication available to develop language competence. This includes the full spectrum: child-devised gestures, speech, formal sign, fingerspelling, speechreading, reading, writing, as well as other methods that may be developed in the future. Every deaf child should also be provided with the opportunity to learn to use any remnant of residual hearing he may have by employing the best possible electronic equipment for amplifying sound." Just about any communication method can be sheltered within this definition, although proponents of oralism have displayed reluctance to being included. Although the term and its definition seem to be admirably democratic, they are of questionable value. What has happened in practice during the past decade is that disillusionment with the results of oral methods in the public school system, increased research on the effects of various communication methods, emphasis on the role of cultural pluralism in American society, and increased militancy by some deaf people and hearing supporters of manual communication have led to the inclusion of manual communication in various forms in programs that previously claimed to use only oral methods. Combining manual communication in various forms with oral communication has long been known as the Simultaneous Method and has been used in public residential schools in the United States for more than 150 years.

Simply changing names for a communication method might do little harm and might even be helpful when the new term has as positive a ring to it as Total Communication does. In this case, however, there are possible negative effects of the change. For example, in one national study it was reported that a variety (it might even be termed a confusion) of communication methods are being used in the classrooms under the rubric of Total Communication, and that there is little consistency in the type of communication used in school and even less between the classroom, the dormitory, and the home (Jensema and Trybus, 1978). It can reasonably be argued that one essential element in developing language in any child, deaf or otherwise, is consistency in the form of language input. Total Communication seems to invite and, on the basis of the Jensema and Trybus study, even to foster, inconsistency of input.

5. *There is no clear evidence for the superiority of any form of communication or language input over all others for all (or even most) deaf children. There is, however, evidence that there are only three systems that have stood, and continue to stand, the test of time and evaluation: Oral English, American Sign Language, and the form of Manual English often used by deaf people and variously known as Ameslish, Siglish, or Pidgin Sign English.*

The studies cited in the section on Oral English, particularly the study by Ogden (1979), indicate that when Oral English is actively and consistently pursued in the classroom, the dormitory, and the home, impressive results can be obtained, at least with certain types of deaf children. The minimum requirements seem to be students with above-average intelligence, literate and highly motivated parents, and a school system, administration, and staff totally convinced of the value of oral methods and highly trained in using them. Complete, or almost complete, control over staff, curriculum, and methodology are required to ensure consistent use of Oral English by staff and students at all times. The staff and administration must accept that years of painstaking effort are required for success. The enormity of the task and of the effort required for its successful execution are obvious. They are also, perhaps, the weaknesses and the limitations of the method. Given the present requirements needed for its success, the Oral Method is extremely difficult to utilize in the general public school system. The conditions necessary for its success perhaps cannot be met there. This is possibly the major reason for the limited success the public schools have had in educating deaf children orally and why they have sought for greater success with other methods during the past decade.

From the studies cited in the section on Manual English and from a historical perspective, we conclude that Manual English is a promising method of instruction for perhaps the majority of deaf children in the public school system. By Manual English we mean the system of manual communication (Pidgin Sign English) used by deaf people to communicate manually in English. Evidence has been provided that, used early in life, Pidgin Sign English can produce better language and educational development than early use of ASL or good oral procedures (Brasel and Quigley, 1977). It has also been shown that SEE-II, used only in the classroom, produced no better results than typical public school oral programs, but that when used in the home as well as in school, results were much better (Babb, 1979). SEE-II, however, is a more cumbersome system of Manual English than Pidgin Sign English, and it tends to evolve into Pidgin Sign English (Marmor and Pettito, 1979).

It is assumed in the preceding conclusion that Pidgin Sign English is used along with Oral English as a form of the Simultaneous Method or Total Communication. (Of course, any other form of Manual English, such as SEE-II, could be similarly combined with Oral English). It is assumed also that the Oral English component does not consist simply of the teacher speaking. An actively pursued program of oral development for deaf children has been provided by Ling (1976) and Ling and Ling (1978), which would make an excellent oral component to any use of the Simultaneous Method or Total Communication. Whereas the Oral Method in many programs seems to mean simply the omission of signs, the Lings provide specific procedures for sequentially ordered speech development for hearing impaired children and for the use of amplification and aural training techniques for developing the residual hearing, which even profoundly hearing impaired (deaf) children often have to some degree.

American Sign Language is the language of choice for communication by many, perhaps most, deaf adults in the United States. Some linguistic studies and some linguists propose it as the language that should be acquired first by deaf children in infancy and early childhood, with English being acquired along with it in a bilingual situation or later as a second language. Although it can be claimed that this was the original approach of de l'Épée and Sicard in France and of Gallaudet and Clerc in the United States and was apparently not successful then, studies of deaf children of ASL-using deaf parents indicate that it is worth investigating. Certainly, the fluency and ease of communication that seem to be important for early language development can be obtained with this approach. Whether English could be developed as a second language to an adequate level remains to be shown.

In concluding this chapter, we refer the reader to the cautionary remarks in the opening paragraph of the discussion section (p. 24). Conclusions at this stage about the effectiveness of various communication methods in educating deaf children must be tentative at best. During the past 20 years a number of studies of the matter have been conducted, and it is to be hoped that the next 20 years will be even more productive. Although the tentative conclusions presented are, we believe, supported by the available evidence, future studies and future scientific developments might refute these conclusions and support others.

3

LEARNING
ENVIRONMENTS

Although the early years of life for the deaf child are influenced largely by home and family, school becomes a factor for many deaf children by 2 or 3 years of age and for most by age 5 years. The types of school environment to which deaf children are exposed and their influences on development are a second enduring issue in the education of deaf children. There has been, during the past century, a shift in educational placement for deaf students from residential school to day school to day class to mainstreaming. Before examining the data on the influence of these types of educational environments on deaf children, however, a discussion of the broader issue of environmental stimulation in general, and institutionalization in particular, is in order.

INSTITUTIONALIZATION

Simply defined, *institutionalization* includes separation of children from their parents and their care within institutions that usually combine the functions of home and school. As commonly used, the term implies that the separation is of long-term duration, such as when an orphaned child is raised within an orphanage rather than a foster home. Some investigators, usually with a psychoanalytical orientation, have claimed that this separation from family results in emotional deprivation that produces retardation in many areas of development (Bowlby, 1954; Stone, 1954).

Other investigators, usually learning theory–oriented psychologists, claim that the retardation in development found in children in many studies is caused by the restriction of certain important types of learning opportunities rather than by emotional deprivation (Dennis, 1960; Hunt et al., 1976). When considering the case for residential schools as one type of education environment for deaf children, it is important to consider whether the retardation often resulting from early separation of child from family is caused by emotional deprivation or by restriction of learning opportunities. It is possible that emotional deprivation could best be remedied by the child's remaining with the family, whereas any environment usually can be modified to provide enrichment of learning opportunities.

Major evidence for the emotional deprivation hypothesis has been reviewed by Bowlby (1954) and by Stone (1954). Both reviews reached the same conclusions: that institutionalization is detrimental to the development of children and that it seems to affect many areas of development but is most damaging to personality. Most of the studies reviewed were interpreted as indicating that separation produces the most severe effects when it occurs during the first 3 or 4 years of life and is long-term in duration. This is important when attempting to relate such studies to the practice of providing residential school facilities for the education of certain types of children, such as those who are blind, deaf, or mentally retarded. It has been argued that the segregation of children in such facilities produces the same types of retardation in development as cited by Bowlby and by Stone. This is a matter for concern. Because the deaf child usually suffers experiential deficit simply because of being deaf, it is vital that educational environments be provided that alleviate the deficit rather than add to it. It is unusual, however, for deaf children to enter residential schools as resident students before the age of 5 or 6 years. This is after the critical period cited by Bowlby and by Stone. Also, the separation of the children from their families is rarely of long-term duration, because the children return home frequently and often are visited at the schools by their families.

Whereas the studies cited by Bowlby and by Stone generally attributed the reported retardation of development in infants separated from their families to emotional deprivation resulting from the absence of a mother figure, Dennis (1960) presented a different view. The researcher made several developmental measures of children in three Iranian institutions. In two of the institutions, the children were extremely retarded in their motor development. In the third, very little retardation was evident. In that institution, modern methods of childcare were practiced and the attendants were trained to give as much attention as possible to each child and to provide learning opportunities for them. In the other two institutions, many fewer and more poorly trained attendants were available and little attention was given to behavioral development. Dennis interpreted the findings as showing that the retardation of children in two of the institutions was caused by the restriction of specific kinds of learning opportunities and rejected the explanation of retardation as resulting from emotional factors.

Hunt et al. (1976) provided perhaps the most informative data on the effects of institutionalization on child development. Their report describes five successive interventions in the rearing of infants at an orphanage in Tehran and compares the results with the development of home-reared American children from predominantly professional families, as measured by the ordinal, sensorimotor scales of Uzgiris and Hunt (1975). Only four of the interventions are relevant here. The first group of subjects, numbering 15, served as controls, and the only intervention consisted of examining the infants every other week during the first year and every fourth week thereafter, with the Uzgiris and Hunt scales. The second group, consisting of 10 infants, received extra untutored human care. The third group of 20 infants was exposed to audiovisual intervention in the form of tape-recorded mother talk and music under the control of the infants, and mobiles that the infants could activate. For the fourth wave of 11 subjects, the infant-caregiver ratio was reduced to two or three to one, and the caregivers were taught the Badger (1971) infant learning program, supplemented with procedures to foster vocal imitation and semantic mastery of body parts, clothing, toys, and other objects and events regularly encountered.

The results showed that enriching the environment to provide stimulating and relevant learning experiences produced development equal to, or greater than, that achieved by the home-reared American children from predominantly professional homes. These findings confirm those of Dennis and others that the effects of institutionalization depend on the nature of the institution and that the effects of early separation may not be as devastating or immutable as once believed (Clarke and Clarke, 1977). If good childrearing practices are followed, if stimulating and relevant learning experiences are provided at all age levels, and if a warm and affectionate atmosphere prevails, development apparently is in no way retarded by educating children in residential schools. The issue then becomes one of whether a particular residential school provides the conditions just listed. Also, if similar conditions prevail naturally in most homes, then why separate the child in a residential school at all?

HOME ENVIRONMENT AND THE DEAF CHILD

Not many research studies have been reported on the childrearing practices to which deaf children are exposed in infancy and childhood, and most of those reported deal with the effects of various forms of communication on the language and communication development of deaf children. This issue is treated in Chapter 2, but a few studies are also presented here because of the relevance to the influence of home environment on the deaf child's development.

Sisco and Anderson (1980) compared the performance of 101 deaf children of deaf parents to the performance of 1,083 deaf children of hearing parents on the performance scale of the *Revised Wechsler Intelligence Scale for Children (WISC-R)*, based on data assembled during the development of norms for deaf individuals on that test. The results were that the deaf children of deaf parents performed significantly higher than the average performance for hearing children, while the deaf children of hearing parents performed significantly lower than the average performance for hearing children. This is in accordance with previous studies by Meadow (1967), Brill (1969), and Ray (1979), which showed that deaf children of deaf parents performed better than deaf children of hearing parents on standardized intelligence tests. These previous investigators attributed the superior performance of the deaf children of deaf parents to the introduction of sign language as a communication system. However, an additional aspect of the Sisco and Anderson study is that the deaf children of deaf parents also outperformed hearing children, whose language is superior to that of deaf children. From this the authors suggest that it is not the language factor alone that determines superior performance.

Sisco and Anderson offer the explanation that rearing experiences and particularly the quality of child-parent interaction might also be crucial determinants. (Although this would not explain why hearing children scored lower than the deaf children of deaf parents). In support of this explanation, the authors summarize the differences that have been reported previously between the ways in which hearing parents raise deaf children and the ways in which deaf parents raise deaf children, emphasizing the disrupting effect a deaf baby has on a hearing family, which may interfere with the family's objectivity and nurturing ability in caring for the deaf child, as opposed to the acceptance and support a deaf baby experiences in a deaf family. These findings discussed by Sisco and Anderson are consonant with those of Hunt et al. that stress the beneficial effects of good childrearing practices in infancy and early childhood.

Goss (1970) compared the parent-child interactions of 20 hearing mothers of hearing children to those of 20 hearing mothers of hearing impaired children, grouping their verbal exchanges into categories of socioemotional content. The results were that the mothers of deaf children were less likely to use verbal praise than the mothers of hearing children and were more likely to show verbal antagonism. The author hypothesized that the nature of the children's disabilities made communication difficult and frustrating. In a study by Collins (1969) of 30 hearing impaired children and their hearing mothers, the communication of the mothers was found to be mainly for the purpose of directing the activities of the children.

Schlesinger et al. (1972) examined the effects of sign language communication in the home on the development of language in four deaf children. The children ranged from 8 months to 3 years of age at the beginning of the study, and from 2 years to 5 years of age at the end of the study. Two sets of parents were deaf, two sets were hearing. All four sets of parents used sign language and voice when communicating with their children.

Parent-child sessions were videotaped monthly at home, on outings, and in school. The length of videotaping ranged from 6 to 16 hours. The children's language development was analyzed and compared to that of normally hearing children. The results indicated that the milestones in sign language acquisition generally paralleled the milestones of spoken language acquisition by hearing children. The knowledge of sign language at these early ages did not interfere with speech acquisition; on the contrary, the number of spoken words and the lipreading facility actually increased with sign language acquisition.

Collins-Ahlgren (1975) conducted a 28-month study to examine the effects of sign language input by parents on the development of language in two deaf 16-month-old girls. The families of both girls were hearing and used simultaneous speech and signing with the children. The development of specific semantic and syntactic relationships were studied using case and transformational grammars. The language development of the deaf girls was considered to parallel that of hearing children.

Greenberg and Marvin (1979) investigated the attachment and separation behavior of 19 preschool children of hearing parents who were exposed to Total Communication and 19 deaf preschool children exposed only to oral communication in the home. These researchers hypothesized that children raised in simultaneous communication home environments would demonstrate more mature attachment and separation behaviors than orally raised children because of greater ease of communication. Each mother-child pair was observed in a laboratory setting with the experimental session consisting of a 5-minute instructional task and a 15-minute episode, in which the mother separated and then rejoined the child three times in quick succession. Contrary to their expectations, the children raised in a simultaneous communication environment did not differ from their orally raised counterparts in terms of their reactions to the parental separation or subsequent period of solitude. There were differences with regard to the reunion phase. The children raised in a simultaneous communication home environment who had less mature attachment/separation behaviors demonstrated more relaxed sociable behaviors at reunion, while the oral children showed resistant and ignoring patterns of behavior. The factor that showed the greatest relationship to maturational level of attachment/separation was that of level of communication competence. That is, the level of communication competence, as measured by the communication subscale of the *Alpern-Boll Developmental Profile* (Alpern and Boll, 1972), not age or mode of communication, was associated with qualitative differences in attachment/separation patterns.

In another study of these children (Greenberg, 1980b), in-depth communication and social interactional analyses were made of the mother-child dyads during free play. Although the hypothesis that simultaneous communication dyads would show higher levels of communication competence and pragmatic skills was not confirmed, the social interactions were longer, more complex, and evidenced more cooperation and positive affect than the oral mother-child dyads.

Schlesinger and Meadow (1972) have reported great differences in childrearing practices between hearing and deaf mothers of deaf children. Deaf children of hearing parents seem to be subject to greater isolation, less acceptance, and poorer parent-child communication. Deaf parents are less likely to be traumatized by the birth of a deaf child and are more likely than hearing parents (at least initially) to provide an emotionally healthy environment for the child and to establish communication through American Sign Language (ASL) or some variation thereof.

As stated previously, there have been few studies of deaf children in infancy and early childhood. Interest in the area is growing, however, and the next decade should see a wealth of descriptive and experimental data on the environmental factors that influence the development of deaf children in the early years of life. From the few studies cited, and from some similar investigations, it can be tentatively concluded that similar factors are important in the development of deaf and hearing children. Affective development requires an accepting and affectionate atmosphere, cognitive development requires stimulating and relevant learning experiences, and language and communication development require a fluent and intelligible means of communication between child and parents and others in the early years of the child's life.

EDUCATIONAL ENVIRONMENTS

Although the home and family environment play a critical role in the early development of deaf children, the school environment enters the picture very early in life and remains in it for an extended period. At present, probably almost all deaf children in the United States attend school between the ages of 5 and 18 years, and a majority probably attend school between the ages of 3 and 20 years. Type of school environment has been a major issue in educating deaf children, and, historically, has been related to the communication issues reviewed in Chapter 2. Traditionally, residential school environments have been identified with a manual or simultaneous approach to the communication issue, whereas day facilities, regardless of type, generally have been identified with an aural-oral approach to communication. Although less acrimonious than the debate on the communication issue, discussion of school placement has been heated at times and seems to be becoming so again with the modern emphasis on mainstreaming, although for different reasons. With the proliferation of a simultaneous approach to communication, the distinction between educational environments regarding communication issues has largely been obscured, and, as a result, the debate has shifted from residential vs. day school placement to issues involving the relative merits of the various types of placement options available, particularly within day facility environments, as motivated by recent legislation, litigation, and psychosocial concerns. The rest of the chapter concerns itself with describing these various options, their historical antecedents, the research literature concerning them, and, finally, some conclusions are offered.

Residential schools, whether public or private, provide both educational and living facilities for their students with few or no provisions for integration with hearing students. *Day schools* are located usually in large population centers and are self-contained units that provide mostly segregated educational programs for deaf students. *Day classes* usually are located in one or more schools for the general population and provide for varying degrees of integration or mainstreaming of students with the general school population. Traditionally day classes for deaf children have been considered to be self-contained in nature.

With the emphasis on retaining disabled children within the local school system and mainstreaming them, a number of educational options have been developed. A summary outline of most of these options was provided by McGee (1976): 1) complete integration or mainstreaming within a normal classroom without supportive help; 2) mainstreaming with supportive help; 3) mainstreaming a student into the general program on a part-time basis, based in a resource room (which is a classroom to which various types of disabled youngsters come for individualized instruction provided by a teacher of special education); 4) team teaching of an integrated classroom taught by a regular teacher and by a teacher of deaf children; 5) reversed mainstreaming, in which normally hearing students become part of a class of hearing impaired students; 6) self-contained classes from which students go to general education classes for instruction in one or more academic subjects; 7) self-contained classes, from which students go to general education classes to participate in one or more nonacademic activities; and 8) complete self-contained classes with only occasional contact with normally hearing peers. Another option not described by McGee is having a teacher double-certified to instruct both normally hearing and deaf children in an integrated class of such children. By combining these options with those previously described, many local educational agencies have adopted a model of cascading services and placement options ranging from total integration without support to residential placement, which, ideally, would take into account individual children's needs and abilities. In addition to the numerous options available, the manner in which these options are organized, supported, and exercised may vary greatly among educational agencies, so that one cannot speak of a single definition of mainstreaming. For more elaborate descriptions of various patterns of mainstreaming and their associated provisions and rationale, the reader is referred to Brill (1978), Nix (1976), Northcott (1973), and Birch (1975).

Historical Antecedents   Residential schools were the first type of educational programming in the United States for deaf students. The first such school—the present American School for the Deaf—was established by Thomas Hopkins Gallaudet in West Hartford, Connecticut, in 1817. The school probably was modeled on the school for deaf children established by the Abbé Charles Michel de l'Épée in Paris in 1750, which was the first permanent school established for deaf children. It was there in 1817 that Gallaudet was trained by the Abbé Roche Ambroise Sicard, de l'Épée's successor. Similar schools were established in other parts of the United States during the next 50 years, and all but a few states now have one or more (usually public) residential schools. This pattern was broken with the establishment of the first day school for deaf students in 1869 in Roxbury, Massachusetts, and there now are day schools in many large cities in the United States. Day classes for deaf children began in Chicago and other cities at about the turn of the century and have been the fastest growing form of educational programming during the past 30 years.

Mainstreaming deserves special attention as a means for providing educational programming for deaf children. Although it is being promoted as a recent development in special education, mainstreaming is a very old concept in the education of deaf children. Many parents of deaf children, throughout the known history of the field, have made strenuous and often successful efforts to educate their children totally with hearing people. Extensive efforts were made to mainstream deaf children in the public schools of present-day Germany as long ago as 1815, in France in 1848, and in the Soviet Union following the 1917 revolution. Detailed accounts of these attempts can be found in Bender (1960) and in Moores (1978). All of them were eventually abandoned, apparently because the large differences in language and educational achievement between deaf and hearing children made separate educational programs for deaf children necessary. It should be noted that those apparent failures do not mean that mainstreaming programs at the present time are likewise doomed to fail. It is possible that conditions necessary to the success of such programs now exist where they did not exist 100 years ago.

Mainstreaming as a recent movement originated in the education of retarded children. Initially, the movement began as a reaction to the fact that many of these children were not being provided with any educational programs, and to the fact that an increasing number of children (including disproportionate numbers of black and Spanish-surnamed children) were being placed in special classes and schools. As Moores (1978) has pointed out, this huge increase in supposedly retarded children likely resulted from testing and placement procedures that were culturally and racially biased. The original concern regarding nonplacement of retarded children was intensified by two important court cases: *Pennsylvania Association for Retarded Citizens (PARC)* v. *Commonwealth of Pennsylvania* (1971) and *Mills* v. *Board of Education* (1972). The resolution of those cases in favor of the plaintiffs established that all retarded children had the right to a free and appropriate public education within the "least restrictive environment," which has been widely interpreted as within regular classes in the public schools. With this, the rush to mainstreaming all, or most, retarded children was on and quickly spread to other types of disabled children. As Moores (1978) has pointed out, "special educators" are proclaiming major advances for mainstreaming children who never should have been placed in special classes in the first place (p. 12). They are also generalizing the concept to other types of disabled children without appropriate prior validation.

The litigation concerning the segregation of educationally retarded children eventually led to action by the U.S. Congress and enactment of Public Law (PL) 94–142 (1975). This law mandates that the education of all handicapped school-aged children is the responsibility of the state and local school educational agencies, and that all handicapped children are to be educated in what is deemed the least restrictive environment for the child. As a result, this law has mandated that each local school district adopt a zero-reject approach to the education of all children within its boundaries. In order to accomplish this, each district is required to develop a local plan consistent with the federal mandate, which outlines a full complement of educational options that may include home-based teaching, residential placement in either private or public facilities, as well as various mainstreaming options— all at no expense to the child's parents or guardians. In order to accomplish this, provisions were made and mechanisms were established to provide for nonbiased testing and placement, the devising and monitoring of an individual educational program (IEP), and due process.

Residential Living   Quigley and Frisina (1961) studied the effects of institutionalization on the psychoeducational development of deaf students by comparing 120 students who attended 6 residential schools as *day* students and 120 who attended the same schools as *resident* students. The investigators were motivated by studies that reported various ill effects of institutionalizing hearing children. They reasoned that the impoverishment of the environment that existed in institutions for hearing children might also exist in residential schools for deaf children and might be reflected in lowered psychoeducational performance. They cited studies by Upshall (1929), which indicated that deaf students in day schools performed better on educational achievement tests than deaf children in residential schools when the two groups were matched on relevant variables and then compared on tests of speech intelligibility, speechreading, fingerspelling, vocabulary, educational achievements, and psychosocial adjustment.

The day students in the Quigley and Frisina study had significantly higher scores than the resident students only on speech intelligibility and speechreading. No statistically significant differences were found on any other of the variables. Further analysis of the day students' performances (by comparing those who had deaf parents with those who had hearing parents), revealed that the better speech intelligibility and speechreading scores could be attributed to what the investigators termed "oralness of the environment," and that communication environment rather than type of educational environment was the responsible factor. The investigators concluded, therefore, that their study produced no evidence that living in residential schools was generally detrimental to the development of deaf children and youth. It should be noted that the reverse was true also; the study produced no evidence that living in a residential school was in any way beneficial.

Karchmer and Petersen (1980) assembled data collected by the Office of Demographic Studies from its 1977–1978 Annual Survey of Hearing Impaired Children and Youth and from a 1974 special studies survey in order to examine similarities and differences between day students and residential students at residential schools. It was found that about 4,000 of the 17,000 residential school students lived at home while attending school by day. About 90% of the students in both categories had severe hearing losses beyond 70 dB. On the whole, the residential students tended to be older than the day students. Far more white students commuted back and forth from school to home than black students, and nearly twice as many day students came from families with incomes of $15,000 or more, than families of residential students. More day students were rated by teachers as having intelligible speech than were residential students, and the students in residence were less likely to wear hearing aids. However, in spite of these differences, especially in socioeconomic status, speech intelligibility, hearing-aid use, and minority status, there seemed to be no differences in the achievement scores of the two groups of students. These findings are very similar to those of the Quigley and Frisina study, even though the studies were conducted 20 years apart.

Meadow (1967) found that day students were generally superior in social development, communication development, and intellectual development to residential students of hearing parents (but not to students of deaf parents). Evans (1975) surveyed socialization problems of 123 deaf teens at a state residential school as compared to 321 hearing teens. He interpreted his findings as showing for the deaf teens "a truncated socialization process due to experiential deprivation which involved a restricted type of communication at home, separation from hearing peers and the opposite sex, strict dating rules and lack of freedom to leave campus" (p. 545).

Farrugia and Austin (1980) reported different results in a study of 200 hearing and deaf students, age 10–15 years, in 4 educational settings. The authors administered the *Meadow/Kendall Social Emotional Assessment Inventory* (still in research form), with scales of maturity, self-esteem, social adjustment, and emotional adjustment. Subjects were 50 public school students with hearing impairment of more than 65 dB (ISO), 50 hearing public school students, and 50 residential students with hearing impairment of more that 65 dB (ISO). The authors found that severely hearing impaired students in public school settings demonstrated lower levels of self-esteem, social, emotional, and mature behavior and that deaf students in residential schools were most similar to hearing students in public schools on those variables. The authors speculated that this was related to social isolation and rejection that deaf students experience in the company of hearing peers.

The few studies cited indicate that the major areas affected by residential living from early ages seem to be speech intelligibility and social and personal skills. Quigley and Frisina (1961) and Karchmer and Petersen (1980) found day students in residential schools to have more intelligible speech than resident students in the same schools. This type of comparison is the most valid means of determining the effects of residential living, because the day and resident students attend the same schools, and school environment is thus controlled, although assignment to one or the other of these two conditions still is not random. Comparisons of *day school* students and *residential school* students are more difficult to make and to interpret, because two types of school environments are involved that differ in many (often uncontrollable) ways besides residential living. Additional studies using this model would be helpful. At the time of the Quigley and Frisina study, there were about 1,200 identified day students among a total residential school population of about 14,000. At present, 20 years later, there were about 4,000 day students among a residential school population of about 17,000.

In summary, the major factors defined by Bowlby (1954) and by Stone (1954) as leading to retardation in various areas of development do not seem to apply to many residential schools for deaf children. Children in those schools rarely enter during the first 3 or 4 years of life, and separation from family is rarely long-term. The effects of residential living on speech intelligibility and personal and social development represent delays and are modifiable within residential schools. As pointed out by the studies of Hunt et al. (1976), provision of appropriate learning experience can result in appropriate levels of development. It is distressing that the lower speech intelligibility for residential students as compared to day students in residential schools found by Quigley and Frisina (about 1960) was found to still prevail 20 years later by Karchmer and Petersen. As Quigley and Frisina pointed out, this difference probably resulted from day students having to function to a much greater extent with hearing people who could not communicate manually and thus having to rely on speech. That is a modifiable factor within residential schools, but apparently, according to the findings of Karchmer and Petersen, it has not been modified during 20 years.

Similarly, the personal and social problems some investigators have reported result from childcare practices that are modifiable. Evans (1975) and Meadow (1976) have been cited as representative studies of these problems. Evans attributed the retarded social skills of his subjects to school practices that included separation of the sexes, strict dating rules, and lack of freedom to leave the school campus. As Youngs (1975) wrote in a response to the Evans study, such practices are no longer common in residential schools for deaf students and, in fact, a number of residential schools are consciously attempting to change their residential programs to become less restrictive. Studies such as Evan's, however, serve a useful purpose in pointing out existing practices in some schools that still need to be eliminated or changed.

It can be argued that any negative effects that cannot be eliminated from residential schools are offset by positive effects. Among these usually are listed the comprehensive academic and occupational curricula made possible by a large student body, homogeneous classes, many specialized services, such as audiology, psychology, and social work, and a wide range of social and athletic programs. It can also be argued that some minimum number of deaf students need to be gathered in one location to provide the teachers and other personnel and services needed for a reasonably comprehensive educational program. Just what that number might be and how it might be managed is pursued in the next section on mainstreaming and regional programs.

Mainstreaming   Some studies representative of the existing literature are presented here. Most of those cited are surveys of the extent to which mainstreaming of deaf children has taken place and how it has affected the school distribution of deaf students. There have as yet been very few studies of its educational, behavioral, or occupational effects. Its superiority to other forms of educational placement seems to have been taken for granted by its proponents.

Karchmer and Trybus (1977) reported extensive information on main-streaming. Their data were drawn from two major sources: 1) the *Annual Survey of Hearing Impaired Children and Youth* for the 1975–76 school year ($N = 49,427$), and 2) a random sample of hearing impaired students who were studied in detail in the spring of 1974 ($N = 998$). It was found that residential schools served the largest single group of deaf students (38%), although that group is now a minority of the total population. The three main types of integrated programs (part-time integration, resource room, and itinerant teacher) together served 19%. Day schools accounted for 11%, full-time day classes for 22%, and 10% were in "other programs." Half of the residential school students were aged 15 years or older, but fewer than 1 in 4 students in day schools and 1 in 3 students in integrated programs were 15 years or older. This reflects what might be a trend not only for young deaf children to be enrolled primarily in day programs, but also for increasing numbers of day program students to switch to residential schools at adolescence because of greater resources for vocational and academic secondary programs and social and athletic participation with other deaf adolescents. Although nearly two-thirds of the students in residential schools were deaf (91 dB +), only 18% of those in integrated programs had equally severe impairment. Thus, as the severity of hearing impairment increased, the proportion of the total population in integrated programs decreased rapidly. Mainstreamed programs enrolled 2 to 5 times as many postlingually hearing impaired students as the other programs did. They also had more students whose parents were college educated and had high incomes than the other programs. The integrated programs had the lowest proportion of students with two deaf parents.

A more recent study (Rawlings and Trybus, 1978) surveyed 1,020 programs and obtained almost an 80% response. The distribution of students was 1) part-time classes and services, 40%; 2) residential schools, 32%; 3) day schools, 12%; 4) full-time classes, 7%; 5) day schools for multiply handicapped students, 4%; and 6) residential schools for multiply handicapped students, 4%. This study confirms that residential schools now enroll a minority of hearing impaired students. It should be noted, however, that much of the increased percentage of hearing impaired students in nonresidential programs consists of hard-of-hearing rather than of deaf (91 dB +) students.

Some important differences among types of programs in available services are pointed out in the Rawlings and Trybus (1978) study. The special schools, but especially the residential schools, had the greatest availability of audiologists and audiometrists. A surprising 17% of all programs (mostly day class and mainstreamed programs) reported that they made no provisions at all for the administration of audiometric tests to their students. Residential schools also had the greatest availability of other types of support personnel, such as psychologists, nurses, and guidance counselors. Extensive vocational services were also available in most residential schools but were available in only about 10%–15% of the other types of programs. Thus, one advantage of residential schools is the wide range of support and vocational services available to their students. Perhaps their greatest disadvantage is the separation of the student from home, family, and the general education system.

Craig, Salem, and Craig (1976) conducted a survey of mainstreaming in all identified programs for deaf students in the United States. The following response rates to their questionnaire were obtained: 63 of 72 residential schools (88% response); 55 of 77 day schools (71% response); and 332 of 806 day classes (40% response). Of the residential schools responding, 30% offered integrated programs, compared to 6% of the day schools and 74% of the day classes. The residential schools having integrated programs reported 556 integrated students, or 13% of their total population. This was slightly more than 3% of the total population of all responding residential schools. In the responding day schools that had integrated programs, 36% of the students were involved, or 28% of the population of all responding day schools. The corresponding rates for day classes were 60% and 53%.

Partial integration was the most common type of program in all responding schools, either with special support services being offered in resource rooms in the school for hearing students, or in the specialized programs for deaf children. Total mainstreaming for deaf students was not common, with only 111 of a reported total of 17,441 integrated students being fully mainstreamed with few or no special support services. Teachers of deaf children accompanied their students to the integrated classrooms on a regular basis either daily or more than once a week in more than half of the programs.

The most frequently reported selection criteria for mainstreaming were communication skills, academic skills, and social development. The reported objectives for integration were consistent with the selection criteria — improvement in communication, academic, and social skills. The most frequently reported objective, however, was the development of self-sufficiency and increasing interactions between deaf and hearing students. Student report cards were the most frequent form of evaluation, followed by informal evaluations and special report forms.

Salem and Herward (1978) developed a short questionnaire to assess the impact that PL 94–142 was having on enrollment, population composition, curriculum, and educational planning in residential schools for deaf students. The questionnaire was sent to 65 residential schools, of whom 58 responded, for an 89.2% return. In response to the question "What has been the overall impact of PL 94–142 on your residential school?" 6.9% responded no change, 31% reported little change, 39% reported a moderate change, and 17% reported a large change; 5% reported it was too early to tell. Therefore, approximately 90% of the responding residential schools believed PL 94–142 had had an impact ranging from slight to large. Twenty-one schools (36.2%) reported that overall decreased enrollments was the greatest change produced by the law and 18 schools (31.0%) reported that increased enrollment of multiply handicapped deaf children was the greatest change. In actual enrollment, 31 schools (53.4%) reported declines, 14 schools (24.2%) reported increases, and 13 schools (22.4%) reported no change since enactment of PL 94–142. Twenty-nine schools (50%) reported decreased enrollment specifically at primary and nursery school levels, 15 schools (25.9%) reported an increase at these levels, and 11 schools (19%) reported no change.

How much of the decrease in enrollments at various levels can be attributed to PL 94–142 is speculative. Although the schools attributed the decreases to the law, it has been shown previously that the reported enrollment declines and shifts have been taking place for the past 30 years or more.

Pflaster (1980) conducted a factor analysis study to identify the variables related to academic performance of integrated hearing impaired children and to determine which factors were important in making decisions about educational placement of hearing impaired students. Reading comprehension test scores served as the dependent variable, and a total of 251 independent variables were selected from a review of the literature. The general categories of variables were demographic, audiometric, psychometric, educational, communicative, linguistic, personal, academic potential, parent and professional attitudes and expectations, and pupil self-concept. A total of 182 students were studied, who ranged in age from 6 years, 6 months, to 19 years, 8 months. Hearing impairment ranged from 30 dB to 110 dB, with a mean of 71 dB, and most of the students had impairments in the severe to profound range. The range of reading scores was from grade 1 to grade 12.1, with a mean of 4.3

Sixty-four of the 251 independent variables were found to be significantly related to the dependent variable of reading comprehension level. The major factors important to the successful academic achievement of integrated hearing impaired children were: 1) highly developed oral skills; 2) high levels of motivation, positive attitudes toward learning, determination, independence, social maturity, and acceptance of criticism and frustration; 3) a high degree of ability to use spoken and written language, including paraphrasing, using idiomatic expressions, and the use of varying sentence structure; 4) artistic and synthetic abilities; and 5) involved but realistic family members and professional individuals.

Regional Programs   Although it is likely that the mainstreaming of mentally and educationally retarded children will continue and that the trend will continue to be generalized to deaf children, several of the studies cited (Craig et al., 1976; Karchmer and Trybus, 1977; Rawlings and Trybus, 1978) indicate that the mainstreaming of deaf (91+ dB) children is proceeding slowly and cautiously. The severe language, communication, and general educational problems of deaf children make full mainstreaming very difficult. A number of states have begun to develop regional programs for deaf students, however, which seek to include at least some of the advantages of both mainstreaming and residential and day schools. These programs take various forms, of which those in Illinois, North Carolina, and Texas are representative.

Illinois began developing regional programs in the early 1960s as a response to the growing problems of small day class programs that had proliferated in the late 1940s and 1950s. Those programs often had too few classes (sometimes only one or two) and too few students (as few as five or six) to make it feasible to provide the special teachers, supervisors, and ancillary services considered necessary for a comprehensive program. Because the educational philosophy in the state did not favor provision of additional residential schools, a series of meetings was conducted at which the regionalization concept was developed and put into practice. Quigley et al. (1975) provide an extensive description and evaluation of the system in Illinois.

The essentials of the Illinois program consist of 1) division of the state into a number of geographic regions, each with a population of 200,000 or more people; 2) designation of a centrally located urban school system within each region to serve as the host school system for all deaf children in the region; 3) provision of a comprehensive educational program in the host school system for the region's deaf children; 4) transportation services for children who live near enough the host school system to be day students; and 5) limited residential provisions for children who live too far from the host school for daily travel. Each participating school system in a region provides for support of the central program and participates in governance through a regional advisory council.

This plan provides programs that have enough children in one location for comprehensive services at the elementary level (at least one class per grade level, K–6, and at least one preschool and parent-infant class). At the secondary level, students can 1) be mainstreamed, with appropriate support services, in their local secondary schools, or 2) attend the regional high schools for deaf students in Chicago or at the Illinois School for the Deaf. A wide variety of diagnostic and supportive services can be provided through the regional plan. The major objective is to have enough children in one location to provide a comprehensive educational program and at the same time to permit all or most of the children to live at home.

Programs in other states, such as California and Texas, are very similar to the Illinois plan. The Texas program is perhaps the most comprehensive, because it includes the Texas State School for the Deaf and has a state-wide administrative group in the Department of Education. In Illinois, and to a lesser extent in California, the state schools are more autonomous, and central coordination and planning are less formal. Although these regional programs have varying degrees of state coordination, planning, and funding, they also provide for substantial amounts of local control through local and regional administration and advisory councils.

The North Carolina plan assigns the major role in providing state-wide services to deaf children to the state school (actually two schools with one administration). This school has, with authority and funding from the state government, established a series of satellite schools at a number of locations throughout the state. These schools are budgeted, staffed, and administered from the state school.

DISCUSSION

There has been a shift in educational placement for deaf children from residential school to day school to day class to mainstreaming. All of these programs currently exist in the United States, with residential schools having lost their former role as the major enroller of students to the various forms of day programs. Although mainstreaming is an increasing force in the education of deaf children, it is proceeding slowly and cautiously. A more pronounced trend seems to be the establishment of various forms of regional programs. These can provide comprehensive educational programs while making it possible for most of the students to remain at home.

Although some studies report retarded development in various characteristics for residential students, other studies have shown that the retardation can be avoided by appropriate modifications of the environment. The effects of the school on development seem to depend on the nature of the school. Nevertheless, the trend from residential to day programs, which has been underway for a century, is likely to continue because of cost factors and social preferences. The regional plans that have been developed in various states during the past 20 years seem to offer a means of combining at least some of the advantages of residential schools and of mainstreaming.

4

COGNITIVE
AND INTELLECTUAL
DEVELOPMENT

There are two related issues concerning the cognitive and intellectual abilities of deaf individuals. One is whether quantitative and/or qualitative differences exist between deaf and normally hearing people; the other concerns the relationship between language and thought (or cognition). Both issues are central to a larger concern—that of the existence of a "psychology of deafness."

To suggest that a psychology of deafness exists implies that deaf individuals possess in common certain behavioral traits associated with hearing impairment that differ to some degree from traits in the rest of the population. This chapter presents evidence in the area of psycholinguistics and cognition concerning this issue. We discuss 1) the historical perspective, 2) the relationship between language and cognition in general, 3) the theoretical positions regarding the relationship between language and cognition with regard to hearing impaired individuals, 4) some research on the cognitive abilities of hearing impaired individuals, and 5) some research on the internal coding and symbolic mediating processes used by hearing impaired individuals.

49

HISTORICAL PERSPECTIVE

Moores (1978), in his historical treatment of the psychology of deafness, traces a three-stage evolution of thought in this area. The first stage was characterized by the belief that deaf persons were inferior intellectually to hearing persons. This theoretical orientation was dominant up to and including the 1940s and was represented in the writings of Pintner and his colleagues (Pintner and Reamer, 1920; Pintner, Eisenson, and Stanton, 1941). These researchers were following a psychometric tradition in defining intelligence and intellectual functioning that relied heavily on paper-and-pencil group tests and tests yielding global single scores as an index of relative intelligence.

The fact that cognitive competence cannot be measured directly but must be inferred from performance undoubtedly led Pintner and his contemporaries to conclude that the lowered performance of their deaf subjects on selected tests of intelligence was a function of general retardation, which, given the state of knowledge regarding the nature of intelligence and cognition at that time, was reasonable. Behaviorally, these deaf individuals did in fact perform in an inferior manner as compared to their hearing counterparts, and functionally they did not, nor do they yet, compete favorably as a group with their normally hearing agemates in many critical areas. Thus, Pintner and his contemporaries concluded that, both quantitatively and presumably qualitatively, hearing impaired individuals were different from their normally hearing peers.

The second stage of this historical perspective was the development of the idea that deaf persons were cognitively concrete. This orientation dominated up through the mid- to late 1960s. This model, or orientation, as exemplified by Myklebust (1960), proposes that there are quantitative similarities but qualitative differences between hearing impaired and normally hearing individuals. This conclusion was based on the findings that, although deaf persons obtained average global scores on individual nonverbal tests or test batteries, they demonstrated systematic variations in performance on various subtests and had test profiles yielding qualitatively different patterns of scores than their hearing counterparts. This led Myklebust to conclude that the deaf child was not simply a sensorially intact person who could not hear, but rather was an individual whose basic experiences, upon which all subsequent behaviors are based, were altered as a direct consequence of the hearing impairment itself.

Like Pintner, Myklebust suggested that qualitative differences existed between these two populations, and thus the basic competence of these two groups was considered to be different. As a part of this qualitative difference, deaf individuals were viewed as being intellectually less abstract and more concrete than their hearing peers, because they performed relatively poorly on various tests thought to assess abstract abilities, such as the *Raven's Progressive Matrices*. In both orientations, that of Pintner and that of Myklebust, the research findings on which these conclusions were based were interpreted to mean that the hearing impairment itself contributed to the differences between the hearing and deaf individuals. This is particularly true of the position taken by Myklebust, who proposed an "organismic shift hypothesis," which was a biosocially motivated account for the behaviors he observed. In this account, the deaf person, in order to know and literally to survive in the world, must rely on his (her) remaining intact sensory modalities, which results in an altered foundation upon which all further processes are based.

The third stage of the historical perspective was an orientation that regarded deaf persons as intellectually normal. Some proponents of this position are Rosenstein (1961), Furth (1966a), and Vernon (1967). Each of these individuals expressed the view, based upon their research, that few if any differences exist between deaf and normal hearing individuals in terms of perceptual and cognitive abilities, and what differences do exist are caused by performance or environmental constraints, such as: 1) the inability of the researcher to properly convey the task demands because of language differences or deficits on the part of the subjects, 2) implicit bias within the solution of the task, or 3) general experiential deficits (including verbal language and communication in general) on the part of the subjects. Evidence for this position comes from numerous psychometric studies, the majority of which show little overall intellectual deficit on the part of deaf persons, and from carefully controlled laboratory experiments that attempt to investigate various perceptual and cognitive processes. Unlike the previous two orientations, this orientation does not suggest any basic differences in competency, and thus ascribes any deficits to environmental factors.

LANGUAGE AND COGNITION

The relative relationship between language and cognition (thought) also has been embodied within the historical debates concerning the psychology of deafness, and the positions taken have often reflected those expressed by linguists and psychologists regarding the issue in general. As a result, it might be useful to explore these more general positions before taking up the issue with respect to the hearing impaired population.

The language dominant or language input hypothesis concerning the language-thought controversy suggests that the child's linguistic development is determined by his experience with language and that it is language that accounts for the acquisition of concepts that are expressed within it. A corollary to this is that, because language differs across cultures, not only lexically but also structurally, there should be differences in the conceptual understanding of the world. In other words, there should be a different world view. In its strongest form, this notion of linguistic relativism and linguistic determinism is the Whorfian hypothesis. The cognitive dominant hypothesis, on the other hand, suggests that perceptual and cognitive development provide the underpinning and mechanism for linguistic development. Language, from this perspective, is viewed either as a mapping-out process of that which is already known (Sinclair de Zwart, 1973; Slobin, 1973), or as an integral and natural extension of the developmental cognitive process and social context (Bates, 1979). A third position also exists that suggests that the two systems are autonomous and independent (MacNamara, 1977).

Support for one side or another in this debate is provided via a number of experiments, utilizing various techniques and studies of different populations. Besides studying the cognitive and language abilities of deaf children in an attempt to resolve this issue, other groups of individuals, such as aphasics, bilinguals, and individuals from different language and cultural bases, have been studied. The latter two groups in particular have been studied, because it is reasoned that if language influences thought or is the vehicle for learning concepts, then individuals from different language backgrounds should conceptualize differently.

One of the problems with using deaf individuals in experiments designed to resolve this issue is meeting the assumption that these children are, in fact, deficient in language function. It has been typically assumed that, because deaf children are deficient in standard oral English, they are deficient in language abilities in general. This might not be the case, because many of these individuals, particularly deaf children of deaf parents, might be employing language-mediating coding systems other than standard oral English, as is discussed later in this chapter.

In the actual execution of various studies of the issue, a number of procedures and techniques have been employed, including forced choice and free sorting, verbal learning, paired associates, recognition, free recall, and other memory tasks. For example, experiments have been conducted to determine whether or not a person's memory for colored objects is because of the fact that he can label it as opposed to some perceptual saliency. In one experiment (Heider, 1972), individuals from a culture (the Dani culture of New Guinea) whose language contained only two color terms were compared to American subjects by giving them the task of recognizing a series of colored chips, which were considered perceptually focal and nonfocal (e.g., blue vs. aqua), by pointing to them within a larger group after a 30-second delay. It was reasoned that, if language influenced thought, individuals should recall equally as well those items that were similarly coded in their language. Alternatively, if perceptual saliency were the important factor, the focal colors should be recognized better than nonfocal colors, regardless of codability. Although the Dani subjects did not perform as well as their American counterparts, the results tended to support a perceptual saliency rather than a codability hypothesis. Unfortunately, this equivocation of results is repeated throughout many of the studies of this nature. When taken all together, they tend not to support the strong Whorfian hypothesis and have been interpreted as supporting the cognitive dominant hypothesis.

Despite the fact that the weight of empirical evidence does not support a strong Whorfian hypothesis, a number of individuals have argued for a weaker version of this position (Schlesinger, 1977; McNeil, 1978). For example, it has been pointed out that there are a number of distinctions made in languages that seem to be language specific and that correlate imperfectly with real world or natural categories, e.g., gender (particularly in other languages) and verb transitivity. Thus, they could only be learned as a result of language inputs. Although it is accepted that the child in his or her cognitive development undoubtedly develops many more categories than he or she ultimately labels, it has also been pointed out that if a purely cognitive dominant hypothesis were adopted, it would require the child to "organize his experience as a large hierarchy of categories (like possession) and subcategories (like alienable and inalienable possession), of which a smaller set is ultimately employed in his grammar depending on the language he happens to learn." This, according to one linguist (Schlesinger, 1977), seems implausible.

A weak form of the Whorfian hypothesis suggests that language does not dictate thought but that it certainly can and does influence it. Most recently it has been suggested that the function of language "is to deal with the categorization problem;...after he has constructed a map of the world through his extralinguistic experience, the child utilizes linguistic input to draw in the borders adjoining categories...[and]...linguistic input may also be responsible for constructing certain parts of the map itself," (Schlesinger, 1977, p. 161).

In like manner, some individuals (Cromer, 1976) argue for a weak version of the cognitive hypothesis, which also recognizes the relative contribution of both language and cognition. This position asserts that our cognitive abilities make available certain meanings to be encoded and may even direct the language acquisition process itself; but, they are not sufficient to account for the language acquisition process entirely. The fact that children develop complex language forms to express the same concept expressed earlier in simpler forms is said to suggest that the language itself is used to acquire new language and thus demonstrates some independence in development.

The evidence for these weaker positions comes primarily from linguistic intuitions and from comparative linguistic studies. There has not been any direct empirical research for testing them. Most of the conflicting data, which would not support a strong language input or cognitive hypothesis, might not, however, conflict with a weaker version of these notions, both of which tend toward an interactional model recognizing the relative contributions of *both* cognition and language.

LANGUAGE AND COGNITION WITH HEARING IMPAIRED INDIVIDUALS

Initially, when the relationship between thought and language was considered with reference to the hearing impaired population, the dominance or primacy of language over thought was taken as a given and the two were largely conceived of as being synonymous. Because this orientation to the language-thought controversy predominated during the time that Pintner was conducting his research, he was undoubtedly led to interpret his studies as he did, i.e., that the retarded performance of the deaf children was a function of their language deficiencies.

Myklebust, while recognizing nonverbal aspects of thinking, relegated most of these aspects of thought to percepts and images and considered the importance of nonverbal symbolic thinking as being rather limited in scope and nature. The relative importance of language in dominating thought was stressed by Myklebust in his hierarchy of experience, in which it was asserted that conceptual thought, or the ability to classify and categorize according to principles, was largely, but not exclusively, dependent upon language. The relationship between language and conceptualization expressed by Myklebust reflected to some extent the then popular Whorfian-Sapir hypothesis, which stated in part that language governed thought (or conceptualization). As noted previously, Myklebust suggested that hearing impaired persons were qualitatively different, cognitively, from normally hearing individuals. This qualitative difference was attributed to basic sensorial, perceptual, and imagery differences that lead to different linguistic development and restricted language experiences. This difference in language development, according to Myklebust, resulted in a reduced language achievement and reduced abstract conceptual ability on the part of deaf individuals.

Many individuals supporting the third orientation, that of the deaf person as similar to the hearing person in cognitive and intellectual capacities, differed with Myklebust with respect to this issue, and many disagree with each other regarding the role and importance of language. Although all of these individuals tend to agree that the deaf person's cognitive functioning and his language development are not the result of altered experiences or deficient cognitive processes (but rather are caused by restricted general and linguistic experiences), they all do not agree on the relative importance of language. There are those who recognize language as being extremely important as the primary medium of communication within society and as the primary means of access to knowledge (Levine, 1976). There are others, however, who contend that language plays little part in, and, as a result, has little influence on, the cognitive processes of an individual (Furth, 1973). In terms of the former position, the argument seems to be that, to the extent that the stimuli, whether verbal or nonverbal, are familiar to the hearing impaired subjects, the subjects are said to function similarly to their hearing peers. The impaired functional status and/or performance of hearing impaired subjects on various cognitive tasks is considered to be caused by general deficiencies in the language of the core culture, which are manifested in the failure to understand the task demands or in the inability to complete the task itself, because of a lack of stored verbal information. In terms of language development and world knowledge, the primacy of language or the language input hypothesis seems to be stressed in this orientation. In the position exemplified by Furth, little attention is given to the relative importance of language, except with respect to problems associated with giving task directions.

Furth's assumptions in regard to the language abilities of hearing impaired individuals, his procedures, and his interpretations of the data have undergone considerable criticism (Cohen, 1977; Moores, 1978); the results he has obtained have not been definitive, unfortunately. Despite this, his conclusions are consistent with aspects of the cognitive dominant hypothesis, which is current in the field of developmental psycholinguistics. Although Furth attempted to establish the fact that cognitive operations exist independent of language and that language is of minor concern when investigating cognition, other individuals have emphasized that language and its acquisition are a natural outgrowth and direct result of more general cognitive processes and operations. According to this orientation, it is the dominance of cognition over language and other behaviors that presumably explains the fact that hearing impaired individuals are able to function adequately in most situations, particularly those that do not require direct use of the core culture's language. The hearing impaired individual, then, is viewed as a foreigner living in a strange land who does not know the language of the host culture. (As with all analogies, care should be taken not to overextend the parallel and to assume total identity in the comparison.)

COGNITIVE ABILITIES OF HEARING IMPAIRED INDIVIDUALS

Just as little is known about the actual relationship of language and thought in general, little is known about this relationship as it applies to hearing impaired individuals. This is true despite the fact that many studies of the intellectual or cognitive abilities of hearing impaired individuals have been designed to investigate this relationship, because the primary concomitant effect of a hearing impairment is a deficit in English language skills. Those who emphasize the importance of language and language mediation have assumed that not all nonverbal tasks are in fact equally nonverbal, and that the poor performance recorded by hearing impaired individuals on some such tasks was caused by language deficiencies. For example, in one study (Evans, 1966), hearing impaired children were administered the *Wechsler Intelligence Scale for Children (WISC)* and were found to do relatively poorly on a task involving the sequencing of pictures to tell a story and on tasks involving rapid digit-symbol association—the solutions to which are felt to be aided by verbal mediation or language facility. The fact that no impairments were noted on the other tasks, which primarily involved some forms of visual perceptual processing, led the investigator to conclude that the poor performance may have been in part a function of reduced or different language abilities.

Certain researchers have taken exception to this interpretation and have suggested that the results may have been caused by difficulties in communicating the directions of the tasks. Evidence for this idea comes from a study in which the researchers attempted to account for the five-point discrepancy in overall IQ sometimes noted between deaf and normally-hearing children on the *WISC* (Graham and Shapiro, 1953). One group of hearing children received regular verbal directions, while another group of hearing children and a group of deaf children received pantomime directions. The two groups receiving the pantomime directions did not differ from one another, but they both differed significantly from the hearing children receiving verbal directions. Therefore, the researchers attributed the five-point discrepancy in overall IQs to the relative inefficiency of pantomime directions, as opposed to legitimate intellectual difficulties on the part of the hearing impaired subjects.

Another study (Ray, 1979) also was concerned with the relative effects of improved communication on subsequent test scores of hearing impaired students. The purpose of this study was to determine whether the profile often said to be associated with hearing impaired individuals on the Wechsler tests was a function of variations in communicating the directions of certain tasks or a function of actual intellectual deficits. In order to accomplish this, it was necessary to develop a standardized set of directions and practice materials for the *Wechsler Intelligence Scale for Children-Revised (WISC-R)*, which could be used with "nonverbal," manually, or orally oriented hearing impaired children. Unfortunately, the results were not conclusive in that the profile was only partly, but not totally, eliminated. The results did indicate, however, that performance on the *WISC-R* was in part a function of ambiguity of task demands.

Additional evidence for the effects of ambiguous directions on the performance of hearing impaired youngsters and the effects of language bias implicit within tasks comes from a number of experiments designed specifically to investigate these effects. In general, these experiments have involved elaborate gestural, pictorial, or other such instructions and research designs utilizing various forms of problem solving. More specifically, these studies can be categorized as follows: Studies into 1) the abilities of deaf children to learn or discover various predetermined concepts or principles (rules), 2) the ability to transfer knowledge of a concept or principle (rule) to novel exemplars, 3) the ability to associate stimuli, 4) the ability to multiply, sort, or categorize objects requiring flexibility, 5) the ability to solve Piagetian and practical problems, and 6) the ability to demonstrate complex logical thinking and symbol manipulation. For useful summaries of many of these studies, the reader is referred to Furth (1970) and Ottem (1980). Some examples are provided here.

The first example is an experiment (Russell, 1964, as reported by Furth, 1970) whereby subjects were required to "discover," or learn, a concept and to engage in a reversal shift in categorization. Initially, hearing and deaf subjects were shown a group of metal tumblers that differed from each other only with respect to height and color. The subjects were then taught to respond to one and only one aspect of a dimension as the correct instance of the concept being taught and to ignore the other aspect of the dimension. For example, one group of hearing and one group of deaf students were taught to attend to color (black and white) and to ignore height. For half of these subjects black was the correct response, while for the other half white was the correct response. Another group of hearing and deaf students were taught to attend to height dimension, half responding to tallness and half responding to smallness. In order to test each population's ability to shift their thinking, half of each group and subgroup were required to unlearn their initial categorization scheme in favor of its alternative. Thus, half of the deaf subjects and half of the hearing subjects who learned to respond to the black aspect of the dimension of color were then required to learn to respond appropriately to the white exemplars of this dimension. The results of this study were that no differences in concept learning or reversal shift was noted between the deaf and hearing samples.

An example of an experiment in which logical thinking was studied is one in which hearing and deaf subjects were required to verify certain logical statements using a symbol-picture task (Furth and Youniss, 1971). For example, if presented with the following logical statement, $\overline{H} \cdot \overline{B}$, meaning something that is both not a house and not blue, the subject had to decide if the picture of a yellow tree was appropriate. Their mode of response involved choosing between an arrow, $\longrightarrow$ (true), or negated arrow, $\nrightarrow$ (not true), which were placed between the statement and the picture. Although this task was nonverbal in the conventional sense of the word, it is clearly symbolic. In fact, it has been stated that the solution to this and to problems of a similar type does require symbolization, but not that typically associated with language (Furth, 1973), except as viewed through the works of people like Bates (1979). In this particular case, the overall performance of the deaf subjects was poorer and more immature than that of the hearing youngsters, although it was pointed out that several low-verbal deaf students performed well, and at a formal operations (adult) level.

In an attempt to demonstrate clearly the importance of carefully controlling the nature of the directions and subject response, a comparison was made of three studies using a Piagetian task involving the conservation of liquid (Furth, 1973). In general, it was found that the more the directions were adapted to the needs of the subjects, thereby highlighting the true nature of the task in these three studies, the more appropriate were the responses.

The tasks presented in these experiments were considered nonverbal, in that words were not used. It should be pointed out, however, that this does not imply that these situations suspended the possible use of language altogether (Furth, 1966a). Despite this, in most of these experiments there was the implied assumption that verbal mediation was not occurring, because the hearing impaired subjects were assumed to be language deficient, which may not be a valid assumption (this is discussed in the next subsection). As a result, the cognitive dominant–oriented researchers tended to interpret their research findings, which showed equivalency of performance between hearing and deaf subjects, as evidence of the independence of cognition and language.

In reviewing the learning and problem-solving studies categorized above, consistent results have not always been obtained. From these experiments, however, it can be concluded that the hearing impaired subjects for the most part do not have difficulty in learning or discovering preconceived concepts in structured situations, with a few exceptions. The evidence for completely normal flexibility in shifting categories, for engaging in multiple categorization, and for rule learning, however, is more ambiguous. For the most part, when structured or provided with explicit directions and training, hearing impaired subjects generally demonstrate the ability to shift their categorization procedures, but when asked to do so spontaneously, a number of investigators have noted difficulties and rigidity (McAndrews, 1948; Oleron, 1953; Youniss and Furth, 1966b).

In like fashion, it has not been clear to what extent hearing impaired children can successfully complete various Piagetian tasks. In terms of their development through the sensorimotor stage, deaf children have been observed to progress normally (Best and Roberts, 1976). With regard to their progress through the preoperational and concrete operational stages, however, more equivocal results have been obtained. Although essentially normal functioning has been noted in seriation (the ability to rank order items), significant delays in the ability to conserve items (particularly liquids) and to engage in transitive thinking have been noted (Furth, 1964; Youniss and Furth, 1966a; Rittenhouse, 1977). The ability to conserve entails the ability to recognize that objects do not change weight or volume when they change their shape, and the ability to engage in transitive thinking entails understanding the following logical operation: $A > B$, $B > C$, therefore $A > C$. Despite these delays, it has been argued that deaf children essentially demonstrate normal abilities along these lines, because: 1) the discrepancies between the normal hearing and deaf subjects are more aptly characterized as delays rather than retardation because the deaf students typically catch up to their hearing peers in these abilities, and 2) performance on even these types of tasks may be biased by certain experimenter and instructional variables, as witnessed by the successive reduction in the gap between the performance of the deaf and hearing subjects as a function of improved experimental designs and instructions (Furth, 1973).

One researcher (Rittenhouse, 1977) recently has tried to clarify the latter point, particularly with reference to the conservation of matter. Drawing upon certain developmental psycholinguistic data and conservation studies done with normally hearing individuals, it was hypothesized that even the performance of normally hearing youngsters might be biased by the verbal instructions and by what the children perceive as the experimenter's expectation of performance. As a result, comparisons were made between the standard instructions of four conservation tasks and sets of carefully devised instructions designed to specifically focus on the task attributes themselves. Both sets of conditions were presented to hearing and deaf subjects. Generally, it was found that the modified directions had a facilitating effect for both groups of children, although the deaf children still demonstrated an average 2- to 3-year delay in performance. It is of interest that the modified directions also had the effect of disrupting the expected hierarchy of difficulty (decalage) for the normally hearing children, and they elicited a different pattern of difficulty for the deaf subjects, thereby calling into question certain aspects of Piaget's theory. These results also demonstrated both quantitative and possibly qualitative differences between normally hearing and deaf subjects in the acquisition of conservation.

The performance of deaf individuals at the formal operations stage of Piagetian theory is even less clear. Although it has been shown that deaf adolescents and adults can be trained or taught to use very complex logical operation principles, their ability to discover these principles seems to be impaired (Furth and Youniss, 1965). The mere fact that deaf individuals can be trained to use symbols and operations, however, can be taken as evidence that deaf individuals have the competency for symbolic thought, but because of certain performance or environmental constraints, they have difficulty in spontaneously acquiring these principles, which is a form of environmental deprivation.

Although significant progress has been made in reducing experimenter bias in exploring the cognitive abilities of deaf persons, consistently normal results on various tasks (such as categorical shifting and rule learning, conservation of matter, and the discovery of complex logical operations) have not always been obtained. This is not to suggest that these events are necessarily evidence for competence differences, because one could argue that inconsistent and lowered performance results were still caused by certain unaccountable methodological or performance constraints (Ottem, 1980). What is being suggested is that the data are less than conclusive.

SYMBOLIC MEDIATION

In all of the research just discussed, it has not been fully established that language was not used to facilitate the solution of the tasks. It has simply been assumed that, because the hearing impaired subjects were deficient in oral and written English, they must mediate by some abstract, alinguistic symbolic system. No consideration has been given to the possibility that these subjects could have been mediating by a code other than an oral verbal code, for instance, sign language or fingerspelling. As a result, the evidence presented thus far in regard to the possible relationship between language and thought as expressed in task solutions for hearing impaired individuals is largely indirect.

More recently a number of researchers have attempted to investigate the mediating process of deaf individuals more directly by using a number of unique research designs. Most of these studies have investigated various aspects of memory and information processing and were based upon the rationale that stimulus items (or information) that showed similar features with respect to a particular coding system should be processed, stored, and retrieved similarly. Thus, each researcher hypothesized that if an individual were mediating either via the visual forms of the printed word, signs, fingerspelling, or speech, then the individual should either encode or rehearse (Conrad, 1970, 1971), associate (Blanton, Nunnally, and Odom, 1967; Allen, 1971), recall (Bellugi, Klima, and Siple, 1974; Conrad, 1979), recognize (Frumkin and Anisfeld, 1977), and/or otherwise deal with stimulus materials best when they were consistent with the individual's mediating system.

For example, in one experiment (Chen, 1976), hearing, hard-of-hearing, and deaf college students were given a passage to read and were told that as they read the passage they were to mark out all the "e" letters as they went along. In order to ensure that the subjects actually read the material in the passage, they were also told that they would be required to answer questions regarding the content. The rationale behind this experiment was that, if any of the subjects mediated or recoded the material verbally using internal speech, then the silent e's, such as the final "e" in "since," should be overlooked, because they have a different effect on pronunciation than do pronounced e's, as in "set"; those who rely on an internal visual representation of the word should not demonstrate such an effect. As predicted, the hearing and hard-of-hearing subjects made many more errors in failing to cross out the silent e's than the deaf subjects, suggesting that they were using acoustic (or articulatory) rather than visual images of the word while completing the task. The deaf students, on the other hand, were considered to be using a visual code. The research technique was replicated by Locke (1978) using different letter targets with very similar results.

In addition, it has been hypothesized, and generally found, that the error patterns associated with the completion of these tasks reflect the mediating codes used, in that the individuals tend to systematically substitute items that are similar to the original, according to the coding system used. Thus, individuals mediating via visual print form would either retain (or confuse, depending upon the task) X-Y and have-cave, whereas speech recoders would retain (or confuse) words that rhyme. Individuals mediating via signs would retain (confuse) on the basis of sign topology, while those mediating via fingerspelling would respond on the basis of fingerspelling topology.

In fact, it has been demonstrated that all of these codes are used by some group of deaf subjects. Although a few studies have sought to compare the relative efficiency of one coding system over another, only one has attempted to compare the relative efficiency of more than two of these systems, i.e., the phonetic, visual (print), and dactylic codes (Locke and Locke, 1971). In this experiment, hearing children, deaf children judged to have intelligible speech, and deaf children who were judged to have unintelligible speech were instructed to recall pairs of printed letters that were similar to each other phonetically (B-C), visually (P-F), or dactylically (K-P). As predicted, the intelligible deaf subjects utilized all three coding systems to a moderate degree and equally well, whereas the unintelligible deaf children relied to a higher degree on a visual-dactylic coding system. The hearing children, as might be expected, used a phonetic code.

Taken together, many studies of the mediating processes of deaf children suggest: 1) that deaf children of deaf parents raised in an ASL environment tend to encode signs in terms of their visual similarities and characteristics (Bellugi, Klima, and Siple, 1974), 2) that the majority of deaf subjects seem to encode printed words according to their physical form (Conrad, 1979) and possibly manually in terms of signs (Odom, Blanton, and McIntyre, 1970; Moulton and Beasley, 1975), and 3) that although deaf persons can be taught more efficient information processing and memory strategies, they still demonstrate difficulties in speed of response when asked to consciously rehearse verbal material using fingerspelling or signs (Belmont, Karchmer, and Pilkonis, 1976, Belmont and Karchmer, 1978). Additionally, the use of signs apparently has a facilitating effect only on the recall of printed words that have high visual imagery. There is less of an effect on those words that have low visual imagery (Conlin and Paivio, 1975). Finally, it has been suggested that deaf individuals tend to store information in long-term memory on the basis of semantic meaning as opposed to a specific code, such as signs (Siple, Fischer, and Bellugi, 1977), as would be expected and as normally hearing individuals do.

Not all deaf children, however, rely primarily on a visual code (Conrad, 1979). A small percentage of profoundly deaf children can and do use a phonetic code, and this ability seems to be strongly associated with academic success as measured by reading achievement. In one study (Conrad, 1979), the major factors found to be associated with reading ability within a sample of hearing impaired youngsters were the degree of hearing impairment, intelligence, and the use of an internal speech code, which in turn seemed to be associated with the intelligibility of the speaker's external speech. There was a relationship between degree of loss and speech intelligibility, but even the students who had the profound level of hearing impairment we have termed deaf and who were good readers used an internal speech code in mediating reading. Although a relationship seems to exist between the use of a speech code and reading, this may be because early reading techniques used with the deaf often stress oral reading. It has not been established whether signing or dactylic coding systems also might be related to academic achievement. Thus, the exact relationship between academic achievement and coding preference or use is still unclear. It is also unclear whether or not deaf children typically use multiple codes and, if so, under what conditions these multiple codes operate.

The studies presented have followed the tradition of an information processing model. This model attempts to explain how individuals acquire, store, structure, and utilize information or knowledge. Other researchers (Kelly and Tomlinson-Keasey, 1976; O'Conner and Hermelin, 1978; Tomlinson-Keasey and Kelly, 1978) also have conducted research on different aspects of this model. In general, these researchers have concluded that deaf children tend to process and store information visually and spatially (or iconically) in a more efficient manner than auditorially and temporally, and they suggest that differences exist between hearing and hearing impaired children in some of these processes. It has also been suggested that information (particularly signs) may even be processed differently neurologically. Some investigators suggest no, or poorly defined, hemispheric lateralization, unlike normally hearing individuals (McKeever et al., 1976; Manning et al., 1977; and Phippard, 1977), or relatively strong lateralization of American Sign Language to the right hemisphere, even at a semantic level (Poizner and Lane, 1979; Poizner, Battison, and Lane, 1979; and Ross, Pergament, and Anisfeld, 1979). [For counter evidence see Neville and Bellugi (1978) and Virostek and Cutting (1979).] With these mediation and information processing studies, possible qualitative differences between deaf and hearing individuals are being stressed once again.

DISCUSSION

In returning to our initial question, "Is there a psychology of deafness?", the issue does not seem to be resolved. Although much of the evidence does not support the notion of a competency difference definition of a psychology of deafness, there are areas of difference that as of yet cannot be accounted for. Hearing impaired subjects still have been found to have difficulty with various tasks in a number of areas, as outlined above, even when extreme care has been taken to eliminate various possible sources of error, and they demonstrate differential use of coding systems. Thus, at least functionally, one must conclude that certain differences do exist. Test bias notwithstanding, it is probably true that, at some level, congenital deafness has some effect on the individual's understanding of the world, because he is a biological entity operating in a physical world. It is still unclear, however, how extensive this alteration is and to what extent it affects higher level processing, given the redundant nature of sensory data from an event and the degree to which the sensory systems that process this information overlap. Most researchers and most educators of deaf children presently accept that any differences that do exist in intellectual and cognitive functioning between deaf and hearing persons are not significant for adequate functioning in society, and that educational, occupational, and other deficiencies in deaf people are the result of our present inability to fully help deaf people develop and use their abilities rather than the result of any inherent deficiencies in those abilities.

5

READING,
WRITTEN LANGUAGE,
AND ACADEMIC
ACHIEVEMENT

The primary goal of most educational systems, including those for deaf students, is to develop the ability to read and write the common language of the general society. In the United States that means the reading and writing of standard English. Adequate mastery of these skills is a necessary condition for development of most other aspects of academic education. Although educators of deaf children have disagreed for decades—even centuries—on what first language to develop and how to develop it, they have usually agreed that literacy, the ability to read and write the language of the general society, is the common denominator in the education of deaf children.

There is one important recent exception to this general statement. A number of people advocate the development of ASL in the young deaf child as the first, and, if necessary, the only language of the child. If English cannot be taught successfully to the child as a second language, then the necessary literature of English should be translated to ASL as part of the educational program for the child. Although ASL does not have a widely used written form (there is a little-used written system developed by Stokoe, 1960), there are other media for its translation, such as videotaping, which is roughly analogous to talking books for blind people. This proposal should not be dismissed simply because of its unusual nature. Similar statements about the need for widespread availability and use of interpreting for deaf people made 20 years ago sounded just as unusual then, but interpreting is now accepted and is available as a common service for deaf children and adults.

With this caveat in mind, it is probably still fair to say that just about all educators of deaf children in the United States support the development of the reading and writing of standard English as the primary educational goal. It is probably also fair to say that most deaf students (according to our earlier definition of "deaf") do not attain even adequate ability to read and write English. Data are presented to support this statement and to illustrate some of the specific problems and processes involved in the development of the reading and writing of English by deaf children.

READING

For deaf children, the difficulty of acquiring adequate reading skills has been attributed, in part, to inadequate language development. For example, Quigley et al. (1976) have shown that the average 18-year-old student cannot understand or use many of the syntactic structures (sentence patterns) that the average 10-year-old hearing child understands and uses with ease. Even at age 5, although knowledge of the structure of language is not fully developed, the hearing child has sophisticated oral language. For the average hearing child with this rich language base, the task of learning to read is that of learning another code (written or printed language) for the oral language the child already has acquired. If the child can "crack the code," comprehension is instantaneous, because the child could understand the message if presented in an oral mode (Quigley and King, 1981b).

The average deaf child usually does not have a basic knowledge of the language he or she is learning to read. Not only the code (printed symbols), but also the language (standard English) are unfamiliar. Thus, the task of learning to read often becomes a language-learning process at the same time. These children may learn to crack the code of the printed message and be able to identify each individual word, but without a solid language base, comprehension does not occur. A major need in the education of deaf children is the establishment of a basic language on which reading can be based. If this language is other than auditorily based standard English (as it usually is), then the relations between that language and the techniques for teaching reading to deaf children need to be understood (Quigley and King, 1981b).

A second great need in teaching reading to deaf children seems to be the development of special reading materials. Most currently available materials do not meet the needs of deaf children (and many other types of "difference readers" also). The majority of beginning reading books include complex language patterns (syntactic structures) and vocabulary items unknown to deaf children. The need for materials that provide gradual, systematic, and repeated exposure to new language structures and vocabulary is documented by research in this chapter. Many reading series include a statement that their materials and procedures must be modified for deaf children and other difference readers (Hall and Ramig, 1978; Carnine and Silbert, 1979). The need for special materials was also shown in a national survey of programs for hearing impaired students in the United States, which indicated that 46% of the programs believed to be top priority should be given to developing linguistically controlled materials (LaSasso, 1978).

These two research and educational needs — the relations between internalized language and reading and the development of linguistically controlled materials — are major topics in this chapter. Prior to discussing them, however, we present, in two other sections, information on present reading achievement levels of deaf students and on specific aspects of written materials (syntax, vocabulary, inferencing), which pose special problems for deaf readers and for other types of difference readers also.

Achievement Levels   No reading test has yet been constructed and standardized for deaf students, so the information available on their reading achievement levels comes from studies that use reading tests constructed and standardized for nondeaf students, or specially constructed but nonstandardized instruments. More than 60 years ago, Pintner and Patterson (1917) used the *Woodworth and Wells Test* to assess the reading ability of deaf students. They reported that deaf children aged 14 to 16 years had median reading scores equal to those of 7-year-old hearing children. This order of retardation for deaf students in reading has been consistently found and reported by numerous investigators since Pintner and Patterson (Pugh, 1946; Fusfeld, 1955; Goetzinger and Rousey, 1959; Myklebust, 1960). Wrightstone, Aronow, and Moskowitz (1963) provided national norms for reading by administering the elementary level battery of the *Metropolitan Achievement Test* to 5,307 hearing impaired students between the ages of 10½ and 16½ years. Furth (1966b) used the data from that study to show that only 8% of the students tested read above the fourth-grade level. Scores for the students increased from a mean grade level of only 2.7 between the ages of 10 and 11 years, to only 3.5 between ages 15 and 16 years, an increase of less than one grade level in 5 years.

More recently, the Office of Demographic Studies (ODS) at Gallaudet College has rearranged items in the *Stanford Achievement Test* to make the various battery levels more homogeneous for deaf students. National studies using the *Stanford Achievement Test — Hearing Impaired Form* have confirmed the reading retardation levels found in the earlier studies cited. One

ODS study (DiFrancesca, 1972) reported results for approximately 17,000 hearing impaired students between 6 and 21 years of age. The highest mean grade equivalent score on the Paragraph Meaning subtest was 4.3 at age 19 years, and the average growth was 0.2 grade levels per year of schooling. The most recent national ODS study (Trybus and Karchmer, 1977) reported reading scores for a stratified, random sample of 6,871 deaf students and found that the median reading score at age 20 years was a grade equivalent of 4.5. Only 10% of the best reading group in this study (18 years of age) could read at or above the eighth-grade level.

These low reading achievement levels for deaf students in the United States are similar to those found for adults and for students in other countries. Hammermeister (1971) compared scores on the Paragraph Meaning and Word Meaning subtests of the *Stanford Achievement Test* for 60 deaf adults, 7–13 years after leaving school, with scores for the same subjects on the same tests from their last year in school. There was a significant increase in scores on Word Meaning but not on Paragraph Meaning, indicating that vocabulary had increased since the subjects left school, but ability to read connected language had not. Conrad (1979) reported on the reading levels on the *Wide-Span Reading Test* (Brimer, 1972) for all deaf students leaving school in England and Wales in 1976. The 468 students, who were between 15 and 16 years of age, had a mean reading age equivalent to 9-year-old hearing children. It is of interest that Conrad found only five profoundly deaf students among those who had left school who had reading ages comparable to their chronological ages, and two of the five were children of deaf parents. Conrad also reported a number of studies conducted in Sweden, Denmark, and New Zealand, showing performance of deaf school leavers at approximately 16 years of age to be no higher usually than the level of 10-year-old hearing children. Thus, extremely low levels of reading achievement for deaf students seem to be universal.

It should be noted that national demographic studies tend to obscure results that are obtained by individual programs. In Chapter 2, data obtained from follow-up of former students of three private oral schools indicate substantial educational and occupational success for those students. There are some studies of students of the same schools that indicate a similar situation for reading achievement. One study by Lane and Baker (1974) compared reading scores of 132 former students of Central Institute for the Deaf, between the ages of 10 and 16 years, with scores for students of similar ages from the study by Furth (1966). The mean grade-level reading scores for the CID students increased 2.5 grades within a 4-year period, as compared to 0.8 grades for the national data of Wrightstone et al. (1963), as analyzed by Furth (1966). Lane attributed the higher reading scores of the CID students to continuous education in the same school with the same educational philosophy at all levels, maximum use of residual hearing, and oral communication in the school and in the home. To these hypothesized responsible factors must be added the socioeconomically elite nature of the student body as described in Ogden (1979).

In summary, deaf students don't read very well on the average at any level. The studies cited are only some of the many general investigations that support this statement. More recently, specific studies have been conducted of various aspects of the reading process in an effort to determine which particular parts of the written message present the most difficulty for deaf students, how the written material might be modified to increase reading success for deaf children, and how the internal language coding systems and other aspects of the learning process in deaf students affect their learning to read.

The Written Message   As Chall (1967) has pointed out, reading tests cover a conglomerate of skills, and there is need to assess various aspects of the reading process separately, such as vocabulary, syntax, and inferential skills. Studies that have been undertaken of some of these aspects indicate that the general reading achievement of deaf individuals might be even lower than the low levels indicated by studies using standard reading tests. Experienced teachers of deaf children are aware of this without the need for verification by research studies. They know that many deaf students cannot adequately read materials graded at the level of the students' reading achievement as indicated by standard tests. A few studies illustrate this issue and show some of the problems presented for deaf students by commonly used reading materials.

A study by Moores (1967) used the cloze procedure to investigate the reading performance of a group of 37 deaf students matched with a comparison group of 37 hearing students on reading scores on the *Stanford Achievement Test*. Subjects were required to read passages of 250 words each, selected from fourth- , sixth- , and eighth-grade reading texts and to replace words that had been deleted from the passages. Measures were derived to indicate the subjects' abilities to use their vocabularies and syntax in replacing the missing words. Results indicated substantial deficiencies in vocabulary and syntax for the deaf subjects as compared to the hearing subjects, even though the two groups had been matched on reading achievement levels. O'Neill (1973) confirmed Moores's conclusions in a study of deaf and hearing children's knowledge of phrase structure. She found deaf students to have significantly lower performance than hearing students on the ability to judge correctly the grammaticality of pairs of grammatical and ungrammatical sentences, despite the fact that the two groups were matched on reading achievement levels. These two studies indicate that standard reading tests perhaps give spuriously high estimates of the reading levels of deaf individuals, even though these estimates are distressingly low.

Comprehension of standard English syntax by deaf students was explored in detail by Quigley and a group of associates. The results were reported in a series of publications by Power and Quigley (1973); Quigley, Smith, and Wilbur (1974); Quigley, Wilbur, and Montanelli (1974); Wilbur and Quigley (1975); Wilbur, Quigley, and Montanelli (1975); Quigley, Montanelli, and Wilbur (1976); Quigley, Wilbur, and Montanelli (1976); Wilbur, Montanelli, and Quigley (1976); Quigley, Power, and Steinkamp (1977); and Steinkamp and Quigley (1977). A preliminary version of the *Test of Syntactic Abilities* (Quigley et al., 1978) was the main instrument used in the investigations to study the ability of approximately 450 deaf students between the ages of 10 and 19 years attending 16 day and residential programs in the United States to comprehend sentences with a variety of syntactic constructions: negation, conjunction, determiners, verb processes, pronominalization, question formation, relativization, and complementation. It was found that, even when the deaf students understood the vocabulary in the sentences and understood the concepts involved, when they were expressed in simple declarative sentences, they had difficulty in understanding (reading) the test sentences. For example, when given two sentences, *The boy kissed the girl* and *The boy ran away*, most students understood them, but when one sentence was embedded within the other to form the relativized sentence, *The boy who kissed the girl ran away*, most students, even those who were 18 and 19 years of age, believed it was the girl rather than the boy who ran away.

Using a series of similar techniques, these investigators were able to study: 1) the extent to which different syntactic structures created difficulty in comprehension for deaf students, 2) the extent to which deaf students' comprehension of common syntactic structures was below the level in commonly used reading materials, and 3) a series of syntactic structures that seemed to be distinctive to deaf students. Summaries of the major findings are presented in Tables 1 and 2. Table 1 shows: 1) the order of difficulty of various syntactic structures for deaf students between 10 and 19 years, 2) the order of difficulty for the same structures for hearing students 8 through 10 years of age, and 3) the frequency of occurrence of each structure in a reading series from Houghton-Mifflin, titled *Reading for Meaning* (McKee et al. 1966). The orders of difficulty are similar, but not identical, for deaf and hearing students. The order of difficulty for the deaf students is also what would be predicted from psycholinguistic investigations of the development of language in young hearing children. It can also be seen in Table 1 that the average 8-year-old hearing student scored higher than the average 18-year-old deaf student.

As revealed in Table 1, the gap between the deaf students' comprehension of specific syntactic structures and the appearance of those structures in the Houghton-Mifflin reading series is so great that the investigators concluded that, on the basis of syntax alone, many deaf students cannot read the books commonly used in their classes. For example, when *for-to* and *POSS-ing* complements occur in almost every third sentence in the sixth-grade Houghton-Mifflin reader, and when the research data show that even the 19-year-old deaf students barely scored above the chance level in understanding sentences containing those structures, a reading problem of major proportions exists based on this structure alone. Similar findings for the other syntactic structures can also be seen in Table 1.

Table 2 presents a list of distinctive syntactic structures that appear consistently in the writing of many deaf students (Quigley et al., 1976). The research previously discussed revealed that such structures, when used as distractor items in the *Test of Syntactic Abilities*, were also accepted as grammatical by deaf students. The acceptance and use of these structures by deaf students in reading and writing indicates that they are part of the internalized language structure of deaf individuals. This point might have major significance in explaining the reading problems of deaf students.

The studies cited for Quigley and various associates and the data obtained in standardizing the *Test of Syntactic Abilities* (Quigley et al., 1978) reveal many consistent misinterpretations of standard English sentences by deaf students. The most general pattern found was the tendency to impose a Subject-Verb-Object (S-V-O) pattern on sentences and to read English as a linear rather than a hierarchical structure, which often led to misinterpretations of sentences. The following examples from Quigley et al. (1976) illustrate this problem:

Passive: The boy was helped by the girl.
Relative: The boy who kissed the girl ran away.
Complement: The boy learned the ball broke the window.
Nominal: The opening of the door surprised the cat.

Surface order reading (S-V-O) apparently led many deaf students to interpret these sentences as having the following meanings:

The boy helped the girl.
The girl ran away.
The boy learned the ball.
The door surprised the cat.

Because students usually knew the major vocabulary used in the original sentences, and because they could understand the concepts involved when they were expressed in simple, declarative sentences, their misunderstandings were interpreted as indicative of an inability to comprehend the meanings conveyed by the syntactic structures of the original sentences.

The importance of adequate knowledge of standard English syntax for reading by deaf children is also documented by Hatcher and Robbins (1978)

Table 1. Summary of performance on syntactic structures and their frequency of occurrence per 100 sentences in the *Reading for Meaning* series.[a]

Structure	Deaf students				Hearing students	Frequency of occurrence	
	Average across ages[b]	Age 10[b]	Age 18[b]	Increase[b]	Average across ages[b]	Level at which structure first appeared	Frequency in sixth-grade text
Negation							
Be	79	60	86	26	92	First primer—13	9
Do	71	53	82	28	92		
Have	74	57	78	21	86		
Modals	78	58	87	29	90		
Means	76	57	83	26	90		
Conjunction							
Conjunction	72	56	86	30	92	First primer—11	36
Deletion	74	59	86	27	94		
Means	73	57	86	29	92		
Question formation							
WH-questions:							
Comprehension	66	44	80	36	98	Second primer—5	6
Yes/no questions:							
Comprehension	74	48	90	42	99	First primer—5	3
Tag questions	57	46	63	17	98		
Means	66	46	78	32	98		

Pronominalization							
Personal pronouns	67	51	88	37	78		
Backward pronominalization	70	49	85	36	94	Fourth grade—1	0
Possessive adjectives	65	42	82	40	98	First grade—4	27
Possessive pronouns	48	34	64	30	99	Third primer—1	0
Reflexivization	50	21	73	52	80	Second grade—1	2
Means	60	39	78	39	90		
Verbs							
Verb auxiliaries	54	52	71	19	81	First grade—1	18
Tense sequencing	63	54	72	18	78		
Means	58	53	71	18	79		
Complementation							
Infinitives and gerunds	55	50	63	13	88	Second primer—4	32
Relativization							
Processing	68	59	76	17	78	Third primer—2	12
Embedding	53	51	59	8	84		
Relative pronoun referents	42	27	56	29	82		
Means	54	46	63	18	82		
Disjunction and alternation	36	22	59	37	84	First grade—1	7

[a] Adapted from Quigley et al. (1976).
[b] Expressed as percent (%).

Table 2.   Some distinct syntactic constructions in the language of deaf students[a]

Structural environment in which construction occurs	Description of construction	Example sentences
Verb system	Verb deletion	The cat under the table.
	Be or have deletion	John sick. The girl a ball.
	Be-have confusion	Jim have sick.
	Incorrect pairing of auxiliary with verb markers	Tom has pushing the wagon.
	By deletion (passive voice)	The boy was pushed the girl.
Negation	Negative outside the sentence.	Beth made candy no.
Conjunction	Marking only first verb	Beth threw the ball and Jean catch it.
	Conjunction deletion	Joe bought ate the apple.
Complementation	Extra for	For to play baseball is fun.
	Extra to in POSS-ing complement	John goes to fishing.
	Infinitive in place of gerund	John goes to fish.
	Incorrectly inflected infinitive	Bill liked to played baseball.
	Unmarked infinitive without to	Jim wanted go.
Relativization	NP's where whose is required	I helped the boy's mother was sick.
	Copying of referent	John saw the boy who the boy kicked the ball.

Question formation	Copying	Who a boy gave you a ball?
	Failure to apply subject – auxiliary inversion	Who the baby did love?
	Incorrect inversion	Who TV watched?
Question formation, negation	Overgeneralization of contraction rule	I amn't tired. Bill willn't go.
Relativization, conjunction	Object-object deletion	John chased the girl and he scared. (John chased the girl. He scared the girl.)
	Object-subject deletion	The dog chased the girl had on a red dress. (The dog chased the girl. The girl had on a red dress.)
All types of sentences	Forced subject-verb-object (SVO) pattern	The boy pushed the girl. (The boy was pushed by the girl.)

[a]Adapted from Quigley et al. (1976).

in an intensive study of the development of reading skills in six primary and six intermediate grade deaf children in the course of basal reading instruction. An extensive battery of tests in auditory acuity, speech discrimination, vocabulary development, syntax, and reading comprehension was administered. Hatcher and Robbins interpreted the results as showing that phonic instruction was of little value in teaching reading to deaf subjects. They concluded that the subjects had not learned typical primary word analysis skills, yet had somehow developed reading ability beyond the predicted level, if phonic skills are essential prerequisites for reading. The most common finding, however, was that the subjects lacked ability to comprehend standard English sentences, and the major conclusion was that the essential skills for learning to read seem to be those related to comprehension of standard English syntax.

Besides having problems with phonic analysis, vocabulary, and syntax, deaf individuals also have severe problems understanding inferential material in written messages. A national study by DiFrancesca (1972) noted a plateau effect in deaf children's reading scores, which also has been frequently reported in studies during the past 50 years. Reading scores for many deaf students tend to plateau at about third- to fourth-grade level at about age 13 to 14 years and change very little by age 19 years. Wilson (1979) noted that up to grade three, reading tests evaluate mostly word analysis skills and vocabulary. Beyond the third grade, successful performance on these tests requires increasing ability to infer meanings not explicitly stated in the text. For example, given the sentences (Wilson, 1979):

> The shirt is dirty.
> The shirt is under the bed.
> The cat is on the shirt.
> The cat is white.

it can be inferred that *The cat is under the bed.* Wilson used this technique to study inferencing ability in deaf and hearing subjects for stories controlled for specific syntax. The stories were presented in speech, signs, and writing. Wilson found that inferencing presented greater difficulties for the deaf than for the hearing subjects, that inferencing was independent of type of syntactic structure, and that the hearing subjects had their highest scores with the spoken presentation, whereas the deaf subjects performed best in reading the written presentations. This latter finding is supported by a study by White and Stevenson (1975), who reported that their deaf subjects acquired more information through reading than through oral, total (simultaneous), or manual communication.

In summary, deaf students not only have very low performances on standard reading tests, but more specific studies using cloze procedures and syntax and inferencing tasks indicate that their scores on standard reading tests might be spuriously high. Studies of various aspects of the reading task—

word analysis, vocabulary, syntax, and inferencing ability—indicate that all of these present difficulty for the deaf child learning to read. Quigley, Power, and Steinkamp (1977) concluded that research and instruction in reading with deaf children need to concentrate on: 1) modification of reading materials for deaf children in the early stages of learning to read, and 2) greater understanding of the psychological processes involved in deaf children's learning to read. The latter area involves the internalized language and coding systems used by deaf students in recoding the printed word.

Modification of Written Materials   It has been proposed (Quigley, Power, and Steinkamp, 1977) that beginning materials for reading be modified to conform more closely to the language systems of deaf children. As discussed earlier, the vocabulary, syntax, and inference levels of commonly used reading materials are too complex for most deaf children. It should be noted that this is true also for other than deaf children. Wolfram and Fasold (1974) have reported the difficulty standard reading materials present for various types of minority group children who bring to the beginning reading process dialects other than the standard English in which most reading materials are written. Children using Black English are only one example.

Research also indicates that many non—minority group children in the general school population have difficulties with the standard English syntax of beginning reading materials. Beaver (1968), for example, found that 80% of oral reading errors made by second- and third-graders were syntactic alterations. Other investigations (Vogel, 1975) have been interpreted as showing that, when there is a mismatch between the syntax of written material and the syntax of his or her internalized auditory language, the hearing reader alters the written syntax to correspond with the syntax of his or her auditory system. In teaching the deaf child to read, therefore, we need to know what symbol system the child is using for recoding reading (auditory words, signs, fingerspelling, visual words, visual images) and what language structure the child is using (ASL, Pidgin Sign English, standard English). These matters are discussed in detail in the next section of this chapter. Here we are concerned with the other approach mentioned previously—modification of written materials to match more closely the deaf child's knowledge of standard English than existing materials do.

Bornstein (1973) has produced reading materials containing versions of popular fairy tales and similar beginning reading materials based on Signed English (see discussion in Chapter 2). The book pages have pictures, printed text, and visual representations of signs based on Signed English. It is expected that the deaf child having Signed English as his or her internalized language system will associate the internalized Signed English with the visual representations of Signed English in the books and with the printed text and pictures associated with the signs. Thus, Signed English is the basic internalized language of the child, and reading is superimposed on it by the association process just described. The studies of Signed English presented in Chapter 2 indicate some success for this approach.

The research on syntax in the language of deaf students by Quigley and various associates led to a standard form of the *Test of Syntactic Abilities (TSA)* for clinical and classroom use, to the *TSA Syntax Program*, and to *Reading Milestones*, all of which were constructed for deaf and hard-of-hearing children and other children with similar language difficulties. The *TSA* and the *TSA Syntax Program* are coordinated to provide detailed diagnosis and instruction in a major portion of the syntax of standard English. *Reading Milestones* is a reading series consisting of 8 levels of linguistically controlled reading books and workbooks specifically designed for hearing impaired children with application to other children with various types of reading problems, including language delayed and language different children (e.g., learners of English as a second language).

WGBH Captioning Center in Boston has produced a publication, *Readable English for the Hearing Impaired Student* (1980), which provides guidelines for the development of linguistically controlled materials and for the modification of existing materials, as well as guidelines for captioning filmed materials for hearing impaired audiences. A major portion of the publication is devoted to modification of syntax and is based on the studies of syntax by Quigley and various associates. A section dealing with the problems of inferential material is based on the study by Wilson (1979). Guidelines for modification of vocabulary based on various studies are also included.

Other special materials are being prepared by a number of individuals at various institutions, such as Gallaudet College, the National Technical Institute for the Deaf, and the University of Nebraska — Lincoln. It seems that a variety of such materials for deaf students will become available during the next decade. It should be borne in mind, however, as stated in the preface, that development of the ability to read and write the general language of society is a major goal in the education of deaf students. Developing the ability to read specially constructed or modified materials is only one step toward that goal. The student must be brought to the point where he or she can read generally available materials. To this end, reading ability must be improved through improved instruction based on greater understanding of the reading process and of its relation to the deaf child's internalized language system.

Inner Language and Reading Strategies   The internalized auditory verbal language of the hearing child, beside providing the major cognitive tool for thinking, is the foundation on which reading and writing are developed. The lack of such internalization of the externally transmitted spoken language of hearing people has been blamed as the primary cause of the deaf child's great deficiencies in reading and writing. Kavanagh (1968) and Kavanagh and Mattingly (1972), among others, have shown that speech is important to reading. Electromyographic studies (Hardyck and Petrinovich, 1970; McGuigan, 1970), studies of reaction times to multisyllabic and monosyllabic words of identical phonemic length (Eriksen, Pollack and Montague, 1970; Klapp, 1970), and other investigations have provided substantial evidence of the importance of phonetic recoding in the silent reading process. The typical reader does not go directly from the visual form of the printed message to meaning, but somehow converts the visual stimulus to its phonetic counterpart in speech as a mediating process between print and meaning.

A basic question in studying the reading process with deaf children is what mediating systems do they use in going from print to meaning? In Chapter 4, "Cognitive and Intellectual Development," several studies of symbolic mediation in deaf subjects are discussed. Among the mediating codes studied are visual codes in the form of print or signs, acoustic and articulatory codes, and dactylic (fingerspelling) codes. These studies indicate that many deaf individuals in reading use mediating codes other than internal speech. Studies by Locke and Locke (1971) and Locke (1978) showed that some deaf individuals use fingerspelling or internal visual representations of the printed symbols for recoding. Odom, Blanton, and McIntyre (1970) showed that other deaf individuals use American Sign Language for internal recoding of printed symbols. Locke (1978) and Conrad (1979) have shown that some deaf (profoundly and prelingually hearing impaired) individuals recode the printed message in internal speech.

Lichtenstein (1980) has proposed a series of studies of the reading process in deaf children based on recent research with hearing subjects on temporary storage of information during reading. It seems that some form of temporary storage system is required for language comprehension. Information about the syntactic form of the sentence along with information about individual lexical items must be retained and used to determine the correct underlying semantic relationships between words in a sentence. Often, information at the beginning of a sentence depends on information received later. Syntactic devices in language that permit propositions to be embedded within (or to interrupt) other propositions make even larger demands on short-term storage facilities. Thus, parsing and combinatorial processes require some kind of working memory for the temporary storage of linguistic material.

During speech comprehension, auditory short-term memory seems to perform the necessary short-term storage functions (Lichtenstein, 1980). Studies by Jarvella (1971) and Sachs (1974) showed this to be the case and confirmed the existence of the temporary storage of linguistic surface material during the reading process also. The form in which this linguistic information is temporarily stored by hearing persons during the reading process is primarily a speech-based code. Some of the studies provide evidence that most readers perform some form of speech recoding while engaged in silent reading.

According to Lichtenstein, there is now evidence that speech recoding or mediation *is not* necessary for obtaining access to *word meanings* (Baron, 1973; Kleiman, 1975; Green and Shallice, 1976). On the other hand, there is also accumulating evidence that speech recoding *is* an important process in the *comprehension of sentences and connected prose* (Hardyck and Petrinovich, 1970; Kleiman, 1975; Levy, 1978; Baddeley, 1979). In general, these studies have supported the theory that speech recoding processes play a role in the storage of sequential information necessary for the comprehension of complex linguistic materials. For reading, the importance of comprehension of syntax should be noted.

Although there does not seem to be much information concerning how deaf individuals process connected prose, there is a large literature on the short-term memory processes of deaf people. According to Lichtenstein (1980), this research has produced three major findings: 1) in general, when tested on standard linguistic materials that encourage the use of articulatory-acoustic storage, deaf individuals have shorter memory spans than hearing individuals; 2) several investigators have found positive correlations between short-term memory span and reading performance; and 3) there are interesting individual differences among deaf people in the type of code they use to store linguistic information.

A particularly striking demonstration of the relationship between the ability to recall sequential information and syntactic skills was provided by Lake (1978). She found that the ability to recall sequential information on a short-term memory task did not correlate with scores for single-word forms (morphology) on a writing task, correlated modestly with length of sentences and correlated more highly with scores on word combinations. Thus, the ability to process and temporarily to store sequential linguistic information in short-term memory was found to be a good predictor of syntactic skills that rely on processing of word-order information.

Perhaps the most interesting finding in this literature on short-term memory (STM) is that deaf subjects have been found to use a number of different codes to temporarily store linguistic information: visual (Conrad and Rush, 1965; Wallace and Corballis, 1973), dactylic (fingerspelling) (Locke and Locke, 1971), signs (Bellugi, Klima, and Siple, 1974; Moulton and Beasley, 1975), and to varying extents, phonetic, speech-based codes (Locke and Locke, 1971; Conrad, 1971, 1979). The actual relationships of these various STM codes to reading processes remain unclear. However, Conrad (1979) has analyzed in great detail the empirical relationships between the use of a phonetic speech code in STM and other variables. The extent to which deaf students in England and Wales used a speech code was related to degree of hearing loss and to intelligence. Most importantly (and controlling for IQ and degree of hearing loss), students classified as having internal speech had reading achievement scores from 1 ½ to 2 ½ years ahead of those classified as not using internal speech. This advantage in reading for speech coders held across all degrees of hearing loss. Moreover, within categories of hearing loss, there were strong correlations between individuals' reading achievement scores and the *extent* to which they used internal speech in the STM task. Those findings raise the critical question of whether a speech-based code (phonics) is necessary for the mediation of reading, or whether the other codes used by some deaf individuals (images, signs, fingerspelling) can also function effectively.

The body of research just discussed can be summarized as follows (Lichtenstein, 1980). Temporary storage systems facilitate comprehension of written English by briefly storing the most recent material read (Sachs, 1974; Jarvella, 1979), and, for hearing persons, the surface structure is stored in the form of an internal speech code (Kleiman, 1975; Levy, 1978). Deaf individuals usually are less likely to use a speech-coding strategy during short-term memory tasks (Conrad, 1979) or to use speech recoding while reading connected prose (Chen, 1976; Locke, 1978). Many deaf individuals seem to use other types of codes — visual (Conrad and Rush, 1965; Wallace and Corballis, 1973), dactylic or fingerspelling (Locke and Locke, 1971), and signs (Bellugi, Klima, and Siple, 1974; Moulton and Beasley, 1975). However, those deaf individuals who use a speech-based code for the STM task often exhibit better reading skills than those who do not (Conrad, 1979). Crucial studies need to be done with deaf subjects to determine the relationships between the various types of recoding they use and their ability to comprehend connected prose.

WRITTEN LANGUAGE

Probably the best single indicator of a deaf person's command of English is the quality of his/her spontaneously produced written language. Unfortunately, instruments and methods for eliciting and measuring samples of written language are not well developed. Various visual stimuli (pictures, picture sequences, filmed stories) have been used in attempts to standardize the language-eliciting process, and measurement usually has consisted of the counting of errors as indicated by some grammatical framework. However, the validity and reliability of these procedures have usually not been established.

Extensive summaries of studies of written language of deal individuals can be found in a number of works, including Quigley et al. (1976) and Kretschmer and Kretschmer (1978). Only a summary of major findings is presented here. The point of view taken by the present authors is that, if standard English is soundly established as the basic or secondary internal language of a deaf child and if competent reading is established on this internal language, then the development of written language should be a relatively simple matter. The written language of deaf persons has been extensively studied, perhaps because it is the most visible and accessible form of language. The development of reading is much more important, however, and development of internal language is most important. Without appropriately developed internal language, adequate reading ability will not develop, and, without both of these, adequate written language is not possible.

Until about 20 years ago, studies of the written language of deaf individuals usually were conducted within the framework of traditional grammar. Investigators like Heider and Heider (1940), Simmons (1962), Myklebust (1960), and Stuckless and Marks (1966) produced various counts of sentence length, type-token ratio [the ratio of the number of different words in a written sample (types) to the total number of words (tokens) in the sample], distribution of parts of speech, and types of grammatical errors. The results of those investigations were concisely summarized by Cooper and Rosenstein (1966):

> [Deaf children's] written language, compared to that of hearing children, was found to contain shorter and simpler sentences, to display a somewhat different distribution of the parts of speech, to appear more rigid and more stereotyped and to exhibit numerous errors or departures from Standard English use. [p. 66]

It has been shown repeatedly that the classes of words most frequently used by deaf students in writing are the content words — nouns, verbs, and some adjectives — also called the *semantic* class, while the least frequently produced words are the function words — articles, auxiliaries, prepositions, and conjunctions — also called the *syntactic* class, or the *interstitials*.

Since the time of Cooper and Rosenstein's summarization, research on both the receptive (reading) and expressive (written) aspects of deaf individuals' language has been influenced by recent developments in linguistics, primarily by various forms of the theory of transformational generative grammar (Chomsky, 1957, 1965, 1976). The investigations of Taylor (1969), Marshall and Quigley, (1970), and Quigley et al. (1976) are illustrative of such studies. Rather than viewing the written productions of deaf individuals (see examples on pp. 83–84) as merely garbled or stereotyped versions of standard English, these investigators hypothesized that the written language of deaf persons is generated by a grammar of rules and that the rules could be described within the framework of transformational generative grammar. They attempted to describe the growth of specific syntactic structures in the language of deaf students, the distinctive (as contrasted with standard English) structures that appeared consistently and persistently in the written language, and the rules that would generate those distinctive structures.

Details of the findings by Quigley and various associates are presented in this chapter in relation to the problem of reading development. It should be emphasized that the distinctive structures discussed, some of which are listed in Table 2, were found in the written language as well as in the reading studies of deaf students. Taylor's (1969) findings for written language were similar to those of Quigley and others. Her research showed that deaf students' written productions, even at 16 years of age, still differ greatly from standard English usage. In general, she found that by 16 years of age her deaf subjects had achieved mastery over some aspects of simple active declarative sentences. They only infrequently made errors of substituting major categories incorrectly, as in *The boy played a happy*; rarely did they disturb the standard subject-verb-object order of simple sentences; and very rarely did they violate selectional restrictions, as in *The rock sang a song*. However, even at 16 years of age, they still had many problems with the morphology of English, particularly with verb and noun inflections. They still had many problems with the determiner and auxiliary systems of English — in fact, this seemed to be their area of greatest difficulty. The subjects made few mistakes in producing complex transformations, such as embedded relative clauses, but this was because they rarely tried to produce such difficult structures. It would seem that, from Taylor's analysis and from the studies of Quigley and various associates, most deaf students at 16 years of age and older are unable to use sentences with relative clauses, nominals, complements, and similar complex structures that are necessary for mature use of language.

Perhaps the best way to illustrate some of the written language problems of deaf students is to present a few samples of their written language. The following are "typical" language samples produced by deaf students aged 10, 14, and 18 years. They illustrate far better than detailed research descriptions the written language performance of deaf individuals. Data on age, IQ, age at onset of hearing impairment, and degree of hearing impairment for each student are given in brackets at the end of each sample.

The boy see a dog. The woman more a basket. The will go to picnic. The family went to eat in the picnic. The boy see inside dog. The dog is sad. The boy is Love get dog. The family and see about a dog. The boy play a ball with dog. The woman work stove for meat. The girl help woman to picnic. The man is run. The man see airplane. The woman is drink. The boy go car. The girl give bread a dog. [10-year-old female, Performance IQ of 106, born deaf, Better Ear Average 100 + dB (ASA)]

We will go to pinic. the woman package. A boy give to a dog eat the bread. The dog barked. the boy look at dog. the boy told a woman stop at car. He carried to the picnic dog sa. the mother told her sister put on the table. She park a car. He was fun. Her brothers played baskeball. the dog played with the boy. after whith. He will go home at 6:45. his mother drive a car. [14-year-old male, Performance IQ of 104, born deaf, Better Ear Average of 90 dB (ASA)]

The family have plan to go to picnic, they packed the foods for lunch. Two children were exciting and will have a fun at there. Father puts a big basket in his car and all of they left the house but the boy saw a dog stay outside and excited with wagged his tail. He tamed and hug it then he took it in the car; They left to the Picnic. Father drove there fabout 6 miles away then arrived. They took off from the car. A little girl ran to the swing. Father and his son played a baseball. The boy fall on the ground and got hurt. Mother yelled "Time for lunch" They ate lots and they tasted so good. [18-year-old male, Performance IQ of 110, born deaf, Better Ear Average of 100 + dB (ASA)]

ACADEMIC ACHIEVEMENT

Just as adequate development in written English depends upon good reading skill, which in turn depends upon good internalized standard English, which itself is a product, or a part, of early cognitive development, so performance in academic subjects is based on all of these. Reading is the indispensable tool for mastering academic subject matter, and the great deficiencies in reading common to most deaf students are reflected in their academic performance, which, by school-leaving age of 18–19 years, is commonly 6 years or more below the performance of comparable age hearing students. This great retardation in academic performance has been commonly known in schools for deaf students for decades. Standard academic achievement tests have been administered in many of these schools since at least the time of the Pintner and Patterson studies early in the present century, and teachers were well aware of the problem before the advent of standard tests. Only three studies are reported here to illustrate the problem, but many more can be found in the literature.

Babbini and Quigley (1970) studied the communication skills, language abilities, and educational achievement of 163 subjects from 6 residential schools for deaf students in a re-examination of data reported by Quigley (1969). The subjects had been tested each year from 1963 to 1967 on speechreading, fingerspelling, speech intelligibility, reading achievement, arithmetic computation, and written language. The results indicated definite and consistent superiority of the females over the males on receptive communication ability, reading achievement, and most language ability measures. Growth in educational achievement was found to be from one-third grade per year on Reading and Language subtests of the *Stanford Achievement Test* to one-half grade per year on the arithmetic subtest. At the beginning of the study, the average subject showed a Battery Median of 4 full grades below the norms for nondeaf students. By the end of the 4 years of the study, the deficit had increased to almost 6 grades. This was the result, in spite of the fact that the mean IQ for the subjects was 105.2 and multiply disabled students were excluded from the sample.

The most recent national data on educational achievement of hearing impaired students were obtained by the Office of Demographic Studies (ODS) at Gallaudet College and partially reported by Trybus and Karchmer (1977). The ODS conducts regular, large-scale educational studies of students in the United States in programs for hearing impaired children and youth. Although the general educational retardation of deaf students revealed by these studies is similar to that reported frequently since Pintner and Patterson (1917), the ODS studies provide the most detailed information on educational achievement levels. A major contribution of the ODS was to modify the *Stanford Achievement Test* to make it more suitable for deaf students. Typically, deaf students as a group perform differently on the various subtests of standard achievement tests. For example, hearing students averaging at the fourth-grade level on the Battery Median of the *Stanford Achievement Test* have approximately fourth-grade performance on each subtest. This is not usually true for deaf children, who are likely to score one grade or more lower than the Battery Median on subtests involving meaningful language, such as Word Meaning and Paragraph Meaning, and a grade or two higher on Spelling and Arithmetic Computation. This makes some subtests in a battery level too difficult for the deaf students taking them and others too easy. The ODS modified the *Stanford Achievement Test* to correct for this and for some other problems and produced the *Special Edition for the Hearing Impaired* of the *SAT*. This test has been widely administered to hearing impaired students, and, although the results do not seem to differ greatly from results of previous studies, they have greater validity. In general, deaf students usually leave school at about age 19 years, with a general educational achievement of sixth grade or lower, reading levels at about fourth to fifth grade, and spelling and arithmetic achievement levels at about seventh grade.

One other problem with achievement testing of deaf children and youth deserves mention. The problem of language development is so pervasive for deaf individuals that it affects almost all areas of testing. For example, scores obtained on the various subtests of the *Stanford Achievement Test* for deaf individuals will correlate very highly, often above .90, indicating that the subtests are measuring the same thing to a large extent. Rogers and Clarke (1981), in using the *Special Edition for the Hearing Impaired* of the *SAT* with hearing impaired students in British Columbia, used factor analysis to determine how many factors (or different types of achievement) the test actually was measuring and found only two, one for meaningful language and one for mathematics, with the language factor being the major one. This study showed that reading level is the primary determinant of achievement in all the academic areas. Reading, as we have shown, is heavily dependent on early internalization of standard English in some form.

DISCUSSION

The extensive information available on the reading, written language, and academic achievement of deaf students shows clearly that many deaf students never reach the level of functional literacy (fourth-grade reading level), have similarly low levels of written language performance, and usually have overall academic achievements lower than sixth-grade level at school-leaving age. The low reading achievement levels are accompanied by even lower levels of performance when specific aspects of reading are investigated. Vocabulary, syntax, and the ability to make inferences from written material all show deficiencies indicating that deaf students' reading problems are even greater than shown by standard tests. Those investigations also indicate specific aspects of reading that could be treated by remedial instruction to help improve general reading level. The low levels of written language and academic achievement are largely reflections of the deficiencies in reading performance. Reading is the foundation of academic education, and without adequate reading performance the academic education of any child — deaf or hearing — is bound to suffer.

Although reading is the foundation of academic education, a well-developed internalized language system seems to be the necessary foundation for reading. In turn, the development of internalized language seems to depend upon exposure of the infant and young child to a stimulating environment with a wealth of experiences that will foster cognitive development and that are made meaningful to the child by the child's interaction with an intelligible communication system used by parental figures in the immediate environment. Because most of these conditions probably are necessary for the adequate development of language in any child, the only factor unique for deaf children is the age-old question of what constitutes an intelligible communication system. A further question, insofar as reading development is concerned, is whether the communication system used can serve as a base for the development of reading. Reading is an auditorily based skill for hearing people, and if visually based language systems are used with the young deaf child, such as ASL or some form of Manual English, then the relation of these systems to the development of reading becomes a critical educational question.

The research on Short Term Memory (STM) conducted to date has provided some enlightenment in specific processes of importance in the processing of written materials. The additional studies suggested by Lichtenstein (1980) in that area and in recoding strategies used by deaf students in reading could open the way to better reading instruction. If the reading of English can only be taught successfully when internalized auditory English is present, as some of Conrad's work (1979) seems to suggest, then we face the dismal prospect that most deaf children will not learn to read adequately — which is, of course, the present state of affairs.

6

SOCIAL, AFFECTIVE, AND OCCUPATIONAL ASPECTS OF DEAFNESS

This chapter is concerned with 1) childrearing practices of parents of deaf children and their effects on psychosocial development, 2) the possible existence of a distinct subculture of deaf people, and 3) the social and economic patterns and status of deaf people. Each of these is a complex issue deserving of more extensive treatment than can be given in a single chapter, but the sources cited will guide the interested reader to greater detail on each issue.

CHILDREARING PRACTICES

In the chapter on learning environments, it was pointed out that hearing mothers of deaf children seem to alter their communication patterns with their children more than hearing mothers do with their hearing children. It may be that these altered interactional patterns affect the psychosocial development of the deaf child and his or her independent behavior.

Hearing parents who have deaf children are faced with uncertainty regarding their children. In addition, there is often an initial disappointment,

which can result first in rejection and later in overprotection, oversolicita-
tion, and unrealistic or lowered expectations. The actual extent to which
these parents modify their behaviors when interacting with their deaf children might be a function of their perceptions about their children's capacities to perform in a number of areas. It has been shown that hearing mothers
of deaf children tend to expect later development of speech and language
than do hearing mothers of hearing children. In addition, they also expect
later acquisition of skills relating to social conduct, but not general independence (Stinson, 1978).

Actual maternal behavioral patterns were observed in a study (Schlesinger and Meadow, 1972) comparing the interactions of mothers of preschool
deaf children who used oral means to communicate with their children and
hearing mothers of hearing children. It was found that the two groups differed on 6 of 10 dimensions of interactive quality. Hearing mothers of hearing children received more positive ratings than hearing mothers of deaf
children on permissiveness, nonintrusiveness, nondidactic behavior, creativ-
ity, flexibility, and providing approval of the child's behavior. No differences were noted in the parents' enjoyment of the child, effectiveness in
achieving the child's cooperation, being relaxed or comfortable in the session, and the use of body language. Furthermore, it was found that the
mothers of deaf children with good oral communication skills were more
flexible, nondidactic, nonintrusive, and encouraging or approving, but less
permissive than mothers of deaf children with poor oral communication
skills. In fact, their behavior was similar to their counterparts who had normally hearing children. These findings suggest that, although the hearing
mothers of deaf children exhibited positive emotional effect in that they
seemed to enjoy their children and were relatively relaxed and confortable in
the experimental situation, they were also rather controlling and directing,
which lessened as the child's communication approached oral normalcy.
This finding of heightened control and direction by hearing mothers of deaf
children has been confirmed by Collins (1969) and Wedell-Monnig and
Lumley (1980).

These studies document the fact that altered parent-child relationships
do exist between hearing parents and their deaf children. Each of the above
studies, however, only investigated mother-child dyads who employed an
oral approach to communication. Greenberg and Marvin (1979) and Greenberg (1980a, b) investigated the effects of communication modality on the
attachment-separation behavior, the social interactional patterns, and the
attitudinal stress factors of groups of mother-child dyads, using simultaneous vs. oral communication. As noted in Chapter 3, the two groups differed
only in minor ways in terms of attachment/separation, and maturity in this
area was related more to communication competency than to modality.

Significant differences between the two groups were noted on interaction patterns, despite the fact that differences were not found in overall communication competency. The simultaneous communication mother-child dyads spent more total time in interactive play, sustained each activity longer, had a high percentage of complex interactional episodes, and had more bouts that were mutually elaborated and expanded, indicating more positive affect and responsiveness. In terms of parental attitudes, the mothers of the highly oral children revealed less trust and acceptance in their parenting, reported more stress, and felt that they had less control over their children's behavior, whereas mothers using simultaneous communication generally reported relative effectiveness and confidence as parents. It should be noted that, despite the anxiety of the mothers of highly oral children, their children were successful and demonstrated no apparent personal problems. Apparently these mother's concerns were generated from heightened expectations that led to a greater desire to control and to anxiety, which resulted in reduced maternal satisfaction and acceptance.

Altered patterns of behavior and attitudes are not limited only to hearing parents of deaf children. Deaf parents of hearing children, too, seem to express uncertain and unrealistic expectations for their hearing children (Altshuler, 1963) and, as a result, there might be uncertainty in how to rear or manage these children. For example, deaf parents tend to express more problems of control and obedience with their hearing as opposed to their deaf children and to have different sets of vocational and educational expectations for them (Altshuler, 1963; Schlesinger and Meadow, 1972). In addition, it is not unusual for hearing children to serve as interpreters for their parents and to participate directly or indirectly in the business affairs of the family at a very young age. In fact, these hearing children of deaf parents are often forced to grow up early, and the typical parent-child dependency relationship at times becomes reversed, with the parent being dependent upon the child.

As a result, some hearing children of deaf parents tend to reject their parents and to regard them as irresponsible (Robinson and Weathers, 1974). The degree to which these feelings are harbored, however, seems to be in part a function of the parent's communication abilities, regardless of modality, with a more positive regard being associated with better communication abilities (Goldenberg, Rabinowitz, and Kravetz, 1979).

As for the deaf parents' expectations of their deaf children, the opposite may be true. It has been noted that there might be greater unconditional acceptance of these children by deaf than by hearing parents. In fact, this was the basic premise of the Corson (1973) study. As a result, deaf parents may demonstrate more appropriate parental attitudes regarding independence and child management with their deaf children.

PERSONALITY DEVELOPMENT

The previous section on parent/child interaction and childrearing practices suggests that many normally hearing parents provide a rather controlled and directed home environment for their deaf children. Given these circumstances, the question might be asked what subsequent interactive behaviors would we expect from the children themselves? In the Schlesinger and Meadow (1972) study, the oral deaf children were rated as being more compliant than their hearing peers, but also less creative, buoyant, and happy. They also were noted as enjoying parental interactions less and showing less pride in their accomplishments. No differences in the areas of curiosity, attentiveness, independence, body movement, or relative comfortableness were noted.

In the Wedell-Monnig and Lumley (1980) study of oral deaf children, the researchers found that, contrary to expectations, their deaf subjects were as responsive as normally hearing youngsters to the communicative attempts of their parents, but that they were more passive in the absence of stimulation and also spent more time in close proximity to their mothers. Similarly, Greenstein et al. (1975) found oral deaf children of low communication competency to show close proximity to their mothers, whereas highly competent children tended to move away from their mothers, to have more eye contact, and to have less physical contact with their mothers. Finally, in the studies by Greenberg and Marvin (1979) and Greenberg (1980a, b), the deaf children raised in a simultaneous communication environment showed less gaze aversion, greater touching, and higher rates of spontaneous communication and compliance with maternal demands then their oral deaf peers.

Many of the behaviors described above are similar to those said to be associated with having an external locus of control. That is, individuals who are characterized as having an external locus of control (as opposed to an internal locus of control) tend to react passively to the world and to feel controlled by it (as opposed to feeling that they are "masters of their own ship"). To the extent that many deaf children are in fact overprotected and controlled, they might not take responsibility for their own behavior and might develop an external locus of control, or what has been identified as learned helplessness. Learned helplessness is characterized not only by an external locus of control and dependency, but also by underachievement and reduced performance when faced with possible or perceived failure (McCrone, 1979). Such lowered motivation to achieve, to seek information, and to learn in turn seem to be related to impulsivity. Alternatively, reflectivity (the ability to check impulsive behavior and to react slowly with relatively few errors) seems to be related to such behavior characteristics as persistence and an adequate attention span. An example of the syndrome of external locus of control and learned helplessness comes from Sarlin and Altshuler (1968), who noted that deaf adolescents continue to blame others for their misdeeds and to lack the kind of camaraderie typical of hearing adolescents. The source for this type of behavior, according to MacDonald (1973), comes from, 1) social discrimination, 2) prolonged incapacitating disability, and 3) childrearing practices.

A number of attempts have been made to explore the personality structures of deaf persons and to explore the existence of the behavioral traits just described. For example, Wedell-Monnig and Lumley (1980) interpreted the lowered frequency of spontaneously initiated interactions on the part of their preschool deaf youngsters as an early sign of learned helplessness. Unfortunately, many of these studies have utilized projective tests, which are notoriously unreliable, subject to interpretation bias, and of questionable validity, and they typically require considerable verbal facility. Despite this, the same findings seem to be obtained repeatedly by different researchers using differing tests in different situations (Levine, 1976), suggesting some possible validity. The aggregate findings of some of these studies are such that the "typical" deaf adolescent or adult is found to be egocentric, immature, rigid, deficient in social adaptivity, and constricted (Levine, 1956); impulsive and unaware of the individuality of others (Hess, 1960); restricted in experiences, confused in thinking, restricted in integrating experiences, and socially isolated in terms of interpersonal relationships (Neyhus, 1964); and delayed in empathy development (Bachara, Raphael, and Phelan, 1980). It has also been pointed out that many deaf persons forsake inner development and establish and maintain a facade or book-of-etiquette contact with the environment (Levine and Wagner, 1974), suggesting an external locus of control.

One area of personality that has attracted considerable attention is that of self-perception or self-concept. Presumably, interest has been generated in this area for a number of reasons. Among these are: 1) a heightened awareness that hearing impaired individuals are of a minority status, 2) the recognition that one's self-concept is a reliable indicator of one's mental health, and 3) a concern about the relationship between this variable and subsequent social development, academic success, and functioning within the normal classroom. Garrison and Tesch (1978), in reviewing much of the literature in this area, point out that a number of studies indicate that hearing impaired persons have inaccurate (both overly positive and negative) self-concepts, owing both to language deficits and to the quality of the person's interactions with others. The authors also pointed out, however, that a deaf person's self-concept is not only the result of actual negative interactions, but, as one study (Sussman, 1973) suggested, it may also be the result of the deaf person's belief about, or interpretation of, social experiences. As for the relationship between self-concept and educational placement and academic success, Farrugia and Austin (1980) as well as other researchers indicate that deaf children in day school settings or integrated in normally hearing classrooms have poorer self-concepts or images than residentially placed students, despite increased academic benefits. Similarly, Joiner et al. (1969) found that a measure of self-concept was a better predictor of grade-point average than were IQ measures for their deaf adolescents. Like other areas of personality development, research in this area has been restricted because of the complexities surrounding trait measurement and the instruments that are available (Garrison and Tesch, 1978).

Attempts have been made, however, to verify more objectively the existence of some of the personality traits suggested by the studies cited above. For example, using objective measures of reflectivity, it has been demonstrated that deaf children in general, even cross-culturally, and deaf children of hearing parents in particular are more impulsive than comparable hearing children (Altshuler et al., 1976; Harris, 1978), and these results tend to be negatively correlated with several measures of academic success. The fact that deaf children of deaf parents who are felt to have greater language facility, at least in manual communication, are less impulsive than deaf children of hearing parents is used as evidence for the role of verbal mediation in terms of impulse control. We have already discussed, however, the dangers of making such a conclusion, because other factors, such as parental attitudes, acceptance, and childrearing practices, might account for these differences as well.

SOCIAL MATURITY

Another area of concern regarding the psychosocial development of hearing impaired individuals has been the area of social maturity. Social maturity has been defined as the ability to take care of one's self and to assist in the care of others (Doll, 1953). Thus, it is a statement concerning the functional status or adaptive behavior of an individual. Traditionally, social maturity has been operationally defined in terms of scores obtained on the *Vineland Social Maturity Scale* (the *Vineland*), which is a psychometric scale scored following a structured interview. An attempt is made in this instrument to assess the degree to which personal and social independence and responsibility are achieved, particularly in the areas of self-help, self-direction, locomotion, occupation, communication, and social relations. Items are included that purport to evaluate the relative social maturity of an individual from birth to late adulthood. The early items on this scale are more biologically governed, whereas those for late adulthood reflect social development and acculturation.

Since Doll's original work in defining social maturity and in developing the *Vineland*, a number of other adaptive scales have been developed, but the *Vineland* has remained the instrument of choice in assessing the degree to which deaf children and adults have been acculturated to the core hearing culture. In general, the studies employing this instrument have shown that deaf children and adolescents typically score below their hearing peers. In one study (Myklebust, 1960), the social maturity of deaf children across different age ranges was examined. The results showed that deaf children during the preschool years functioned much like their hearing peers, but the older children functioned at much lower levels, suggesting that the discrepancy in social maturity between hearing and deaf persons increased with age. The researcher concluded that this increasing gap in social maturity was primarily because of a deficit in knowing and using various forms of standard English. This explanation seems reasonable, because many items scored at the adult level on the *Vineland* implicitly involve the use of some form of standard English.

Social functioning is a complex phenomenon and there may be numerous reasons why an individual might not achieve social maturity besides a lack of standard English. Among these are childrearing practices and various parental attitudes that might mitigate against the development of independence, e.g., overprotectiveness. It is suggested earlier in this chapter and in the chapter "Language and Communication Methods" that parental attitudes and acceptance of the child might be as important a factor in encouraging personality and language development in deaf children as the use of a specific communication methodology (Corson, 1973). The same can be said of the development of social maturity. Schlesinger and Meadow (1972) found that, for a group of orally raised deaf children, the quality of parent-child communication was significantly related to the children's social maturity.

Another possible source of influence in the development of social maturity in a deaf child is the type of school and living environment to which the child is exposed. Early studies suggested that children from residential schools were less socially mature than those from day schools. Recently this has been reconfirmed by Quarrington and Solomon (1975) who found that rare home visiting of residential deaf students was associated with lower social maturity, more so than in students either living at home or living at a residential school with frequent home visits. This was particularly true in the areas of self-direction, locomotion, and self-help. They also found that the judgments of social maturity elicited from residential school house parents were systematically lower and less variable across children than parental judgments, suggesting that many house parents operate from a stereotypic perspective.

BEHAVIORAL PROBLEMS AND MENTAL HEALTH PROGRAMS

Inasmuch as the early development of the deaf child can be more turbulent than that of most hearing children, as well as being characterized by altered or disrupted parent-child relationships, insufficient socialization opportunities, possible identity crises, and the possibility of a poorly integrated personality structure, there exists the possibility of a higher incidence of behavioral and emotional problems; however, there is conflicting evidence on this matter. The figures for the school-age population range from 8.4% (Meadow and Trybus, 1979) to more than 30% (Schlesinger and Meadow, 1972). The differences in incidence figures could in part be caused by differences in defining what was meant by a behavior problem and other methodological difficulties. In general, however, most surveys tend to suggest that there are more behavioral problems and emotional disturbance in the school-age deaf population than in the school-age hearing population.

At the adult level, it has been noted that the incidence rate of schizophrenia is not appreciably different between the deaf and hearing populations, but that deaf persons present a higher incidence of "problems of living." (Rainer and Altshuler, 1966). Although criminal/delinquency incidence figures are not available, it has been noted that all types of criminal violations are committed by deaf people and primarily by low socioeconomic status single deaf persons of hearing parents. Crimes of a sexual nature seem to predominate (Klaber and Falek, 1963).

To date, there have been only a few mental health programs outside of educational settings established to provide services for deaf individuals, particularly for children. Among those programs, three have become well known for their services, primarily because of their pioneering efforts in this area, and each is staffed by individuals who have specialized in the treatment of deaf patients. These three facilities are the outpatient facility at the Columbia Presbyterian Hospital in New York City, with its sister inpatient facility at Rockland State Hospital; the St. Elizabeth Hospital program in Washington, D.C.; and the facilities at the Langley Porter Hospital in San Francisco, California. Each of these facilities offers various forms of direct and supportive mental health programs. Although the number of educational programs for behaviorally disordered children is increasing, particularly at residential schools, the overall provision for mental health services through extramural agencies has developed slowly because of 1) hesitancy on the part of these agencies, 2) the lack of training programs to prepare mental health personnel to work with this population, and 3) the general trend toward community-based, decentralized mental health centers.

THE SUBCULTURE OF DEAF PEOPLE

A subculture refers to the "...cultural patterns of a subsociety which contains both sexes, all ages, and family groups, which parallels the larger society in that it provides for a network of groups and institutions extending throughout the individual's entire life cycle." (Gordon, 1970 p. 154). Functionally, such a group provides for group self-identification and institutions that permit relationships with other primary members of the group. The critical features of a subculture or subsociety are: 1) that it be comprised of a group of individuals who form a cohesive group that permits self-identification and who have a common set of values and beliefs, 2) that it permit primary relationships with other members of the group to be established and maintained throughout one's life cycle, and 3) that it possess institutionalized social and informational networks and a heritage — all of which are perpetuated over time. These definitions and characteristics define only ideal types. Few cases identified as subcultures actually satisfy all these criteria completely, and thus this concept should be considered as relative rather than absolute (Demerath and Maxwell, 1976).

Because subcultures result from multiple factors, any given group defined by a single feature, such as race, is in actuality a heterogeneous group. Recently, it has been suggested that the dimension of handicap, or more specifically, deafness, should be added to the list of factors defining subcultures, because at least in the case of deaf persons, this population is fairly heterogeneous, but yet has sufficient cohesiveness to qualify it as a legitimate defining variable. It is our purpose to explore this notion as applied to the deaf population.

Historical Antecedents   Sociology as a field of study is itself a relatively recent discipline. To speak of a sociology of deafness, then, is to speak of an even more recent phenomenon, because studies in this area utilize techniques and procedures from general sociology. It has not been until comparatively recently that formal attempts have been made to study the deaf population sociologically, and much of this research has been descriptive and demographic in nature. Initially, these studies were primarily incidence surveys. More recently (during the last 50 years) attempts have been made to describe in more detail some aspects of this population.

Probably the earliest formal research effort of this type was conducted by Best in 1943. In that study, attempts were made to collect and present data on the incidence of deafness and demographics on race, age, mental and physical conditions, marriage, procreation, educational status, communication use, economic status, social organizations, organizations concerned with deafness, educational provisions for deaf children, and the legal treatment and rights of deaf persons. Since that time, other studies of a national or regional nature have been conducted that have described various sociological patterns associated with the deaf population. Some of the findings are presented here.

Occupational and Economic Status   A number of research projects have attempted to document the economic and occupational status of the deaf population, and they all have produced similar findings. This population can be described as being a stable but underemployed segment of the work force, whose members are employed primarily in skilled or semiskilled trades. At least this is true for the white male portion of the population. Although deaf individuals have been found to hold positions in almost every broad job category (Lunde and Bigman, 1959), the majority are employed in private industries, particularly as machine operators or as craftsmen in the manufacturing of nondurable goods. In fact, a recent study revealed that approximately 46% of the deaf population was employed within the manufacturing industry and 60% of all deaf persons were employed in either skilled or semiskilled trades (Schein and Delk, 1974). Even within postsecondary vocational-technical training programs for deaf persons, the occupational choices tend to be along traditional and sex-typed lines, e.g., printing, carpentry, and general office work (Moores, 1979).

In the Schein and Delk study, it was also reported that the occupational and economic status of nonwhites was not as good as that of whites. (This, of course, is true also for the general population.) Although the unemployment rate for white deaf males and females was less than the rate for the general population, the nonwhite deaf males were reported to have an unemployment rate five times that of white deaf males, i.e., around 11%. Nonwhite deaf females were reported to have an unemployment rate twice that of white deaf women, i.e., around 16%. These unemployment differences were even greater than those reported for the general population. Additional support for the conclusion that nonwhite deaf persons typically suffer both unemployment and underemployment comes from a study of black deaf adults in the Watts area of Los Angeles (Smith, 1972). These racial differences are not only manifested occupationally, but they are also manifested economically, educationally, and socially.

The incomes of families with deaf heads of households were found to be lower than for the general population, with families headed by nonwhite deaf males earning less than those with white deaf males, followed by white females and nonwhite deaf females (Schein and Delk, 1974). Not only were family incomes noted to be lower, but individual incomes of deaf persons were only about 74% of those of normally hearing individuals. Further evidence for the fact that many deaf persons are underemployed comes from data provided by Schein and Delk in their study. It was noted that 43% of those deaf persons who had one or more years of higher education had principal occupations that could be categorized as being below their level of preparation. In addition, although deaf persons have been found to be highly stable employees (employees of the same firm for periods greater than 3 to 7 years), this rarely is rewarded or translated into job promotions (Lunde and Bigman, 1959; Altshuler and Baroff, 1963). That deaf individuals typically are underemployed undoubtedly is the result of a number of factors, among which are: 1) employer prejudice, 2) a lack of vocational information, and 3) reduced language and educational achievement.

Employer Prejudice   A number of research projects have been conducted to investigate various aspects of employer attitude. It has been found that employers are prejudiced against hiring handicapped individuals and that the strength of these prejudicial attitudes varies as a function of the different types of disabilities. The hearing impaired, for example, have been found to be more acceptable as employees that epileptics, ex-mental patients, and ex-prisoners, but less so than nonambulatory persons or persons discharged from a tuberculosis sanitorium (Richard, Triandes, and Patterson, 1963). Similarly, judgments by school administrators regarding the suitability of various disabilities for a third-grade teaching assignment revealed that a deaf applicant was rated worse than all other disabilities, except epileptics. It has also been found that 1) a discrepancy often exists between employers' expressed opinions in regard to hiring disabled persons and their actual hiring practices (Jennings, 1951), and that 2) the attitude and hiring practices of various employers vary as a function of the experience that the industry has had with other disabled persons (Furfey and Harte, 1968). Those who have had little or no experience with disabled individuals expressed concern or reluctance in hiring such individuals, and those who were experienced in this area often expressed preference for disabled and, in particular, for deaf workers.

Certain prejudicial attitudes and stereotypes of potential employers regarding deaf workers are manifested in various excuses for not hiring a disabled person and in the expression of a limited range of possible jobs suitable for any given group of handicapped individuals. The primary reasons given for not hiring a deaf individual generally involve safety and matters regarding job efficiency and communication (Harvey and Luongo, 1945; the Federation Employment and Guidance Service, 1959; Furfey and Harte, 1968; Phillips, 1979). Closely associated with these findings are the additional findings that employers not familiar with deaf individuals tend to restrict the possible scope of jobs that would be suitable for this population (Furfey and Harte, 1968; Pino, 1970; Phillips, 1975a, b). Naive employers often believe that a deaf person is best suited for bench work, the machine trades, processing data, and clerical jobs—all of which are repetitive and involve little language ability. Most employers are reticent to put a deaf person in a supervisory position, and they often lack information regarding specific problems a deaf worker may encounter in seeking for and performing a job.

Lack of Vocational Information   Evidence that deaf persons have impoverished vocational information, which may lead to underemployment, comes from a study designed to investigate the vocational development of deaf adolescents (Lerman and Guilfoyle, 1970). In this study an attempt was made to investigate the development of vocational interests and planning abilities of deaf youth, ages 12.5 to 20.5 years, and to establish the determinants of their vocational maturity. Vocational maturity as defined by these researchers was the degree to which individuals expressed vocational goals that were realistic, independently determined, and consonant with their abilities and with the degree to which they possessed specific information regarding these vocational goals. In general, the deaf subjects were found to choose jobs at a lower socioeconomic level than their hearing peers, and these chosen occupations tended to cluster at the semiskilled and unskilled levels. These deaf students particularly chose occupations that were typically classified as traditional jobs that deaf persons pursue, such as printing. These findings are almost identical to a second study investigating the occupational plans and aspirations of deaf adolescents (Joiner, Erickson, and Crittenden, 1968).

The findings led the researchers to conclude that a communication network existed, flowing from deaf adults to older deaf students to younger deaf students, that was independent of school and familial influences. They also concluded that this information network, unfortunately, did not provide information regarding a wide range of possible vocational opportunities. In fact, it was discovered that, for the most part, deaf adolescents had a very limited fund of information regarding the work-a-day world as a result of restricted sources of information and a restricted ability to process information because of language difficulties. These results also suggest that typical vocational programs for deaf youth might not provide them with sufficient vocational information for making good career choices.

This idea that traditional vocational training programs are inadequate finds support in one study, in which 60% to 80% of deaf persons in the work force reported not following the trade for which they were originally trained (Lunde and Bigman, 1959). As a result, it has been suggested that vocational training programs change their focus from specific skill training to one that provides students with more generic informational and work skills (Lerman and Guilfoyle, 1970). Additional support for this notion comes from the fact that these traditional jobs are being phased out with our growing technology and with the general shift in the employment sector to service-type positions.

As might be expected, vocational information acquisition and vocational planning by deaf youth was found to be related to their language and communication competence, to the level of cultural and educational stimulation in their homes, and, to a lesser extent, to intelligence and independent living skills (Lerman and Guilfoyle, 1970). To some degree these same factors, in addition to the factors of degree of hearing impairment, level of functional achievement, and age at onset, have been found to be associated with actual occupational attainment and economic status (Lunde and Bigman, 1959; Altshuler and Baroff, 1963; Schein and Delk, 1974). In general, those with less hearing impairment, a later age at onset, and higher levels of educational achievement tended to obtain occupations providing greater economic benefits.

Reduced Language and Educational Achievement   Finally, evidence for the fact that the hearing impaired population's general occupation level and reduced economic status is related to their general language deficits and academic achievement is straightforward. Less than 10% of the hearing impaired population is employed in professional or technical fields requiring advanced educational achievement and even fewer are in service- and sales-related activities requiring good oral and written communication skills. As for their underemployment in this respect, many deaf persons are found to be employed in jobs that would be considered below their level of education or training (Schein and Delk, 1974).

With regard to job satisfaction, the majority of deaf persons studied typically have given positive responses, or at least have not openly expressed dissatisfaction. On the other hand, a significant number of these individuals, 68%, feel they have been discriminated against at one time or another. As a result, these attitudes might more accurately be described as complacency rather than satisfaction. Of those who openly expressed dissatisfaction, many were, in the opinion of the researchers, disturbed by their hearing impairment. These persons also tended to have interpersonal problems with their employers (Altshuler and Baroff, 1963) or were blacks from ghetto situations who presumably were disturbed by their lot in life (Smith, 1972). As for their preference in co-workers, one study (Altshuler and Baroff, 1963) has suggested that a significant number of deaf workers (45%) prefer to work only with hearing individuals, while a nearly equal number (41%) expressed no preference as to hearing status of their co-workers. Only a small percentage (11%) of the sample studied expressed a distinct preference for working only with deaf individuals. Of those who preferred not to work with other deaf persons, more than 50% gave reasons that could be regarded as prejudicial in nature.

Social and Leisure Activities   Despite the fact that many deaf individuals seem to prefer not to work with other deaf individuals, this is not the case in their socialization patterns. In one study (Baroff, 1963), it was determined that most deaf people have an active social life, mostly with other deaf individuals. A significant number of deaf adults (45%), however, did report socializing with hearing individuals as well.

Although this socialization occurs on an individual level, there also exists an extensive network of social groups and organizations designed for and by deaf people themselves, which is unlike any of the other disability groups. Among these social groups are the National Association of the Deaf (NAD), with its state and local chapters and auxiliary organizations (the Junior NAD), the Fraternal Society of the Deaf, and the Deaf Olympics. In addition to these national societies, there exist numerous local clubs and organizations, often sponsored by religious or other groups or by deaf people themselves. Recently, many cities in which there are large concentrations of deaf individuals have developed community communication centers. These centers have been established so that deaf persons might give and receive personal and business messages. In one respect, they are like answering services for those who own a telecommunication device (TTY), which permits hearing impaired persons to communicate via a telephone by means of a machine that translates a typed message into sound/electrical impulses. These centers also assist deaf persons in communicating with the hearing population, either by phone or interpreter. Because these centers tend to be focal points of communication within the community of deaf people and because they provide guidance and entry into various community agencies, they have been assimilated into the social network of the deaf population.

Numerous deaf persons, either by chance or by choice, do not belong to any social group and do not socialize with other deaf persons to any extent. This is true of some orally successful deaf people who become assimilated in the general society. It is particularly true, but for the opposite reason, of black and other minorities. These individuals are typically not represented in the organizations of deaf people, which suggests that some form of *de facto* segregation or overt discrimination is in operation. Although these minorities sometimes have organizations of their own, the social network within these minorities is far less formal than for the deaf white population, and in some ghetto situations, is nonexistent (Smith, 1972).

Other than participation in social organizations and social organization–sponsored activities, little else is known, from an empirical point of view, about deaf people's use of other leisure activities. It has been found that newspapers and magazines are the most popular reading material used by deaf persons (McLaughlin and Andrews, 1975), and that roughly 79% of the population read a newspaper once a day (Baroff, 1963). Other leisure-time activities enjoyed by deaf persons are sports, watching (captioned) television, watching specially captioned movies (generally at a club for deaf persons), and, more recently, attending or participating in dramatic plays or signing choral groups. It should be pointed out that, for the last two activities, the materials used are usually adaptions of plays and songs written by hearing individuals. There are few plays or songs written by congenitally deaf individuals themselves.

Sexual Patterns and Family Studies   Knowledge about the sexual patterns and activities of hearing impaired individuals is limited; however, one large study was conducted in conjunction with a state-wide survey of the mental health problems of deaf persons (Altshuler, 1963). In reporting the data, the researcher noted that many of the subjects were from residential school environments and cautioned that, because of the sensitive nature of the questions asked, the subjects might not always have answered the ques-

tions honestly. The results of this study suggest that these subjects partici-
pated in very little actual heterosexual activity while they were in school. In
fact, there was more homosexual activity, possibly of a transitory nature,
than heterosexual activity. This, it was felt, was probably because of restrictive policies of some residential schools. This idea of socio-sexual restriction
during adolescence is supported by the fact that more than one-half of the
subjects reported never having dated the opposite sex, and 10% reported
having no friends of the opposite sex during their school years. Among those
who eventually married, 30% had no special boy- or girlfriend prior to their
spouse, and 16% only dated in groups. These behavioral patterns, according to the researcher, were more prevalent among older than among younger
deaf individuals, indicating that the patterns were changing. Yet today one
in three residential programs for deaf students still do not provide for sex
education, and, for those that do have a program, the quality varies (Fitz-
Gerald and Fitz-Gerald, 1976).

The incidence figures for marriage have increased over time, although
they are still reported to be below the national average. At the turn of the
century the incidence figure was approximately 30% of the deaf population, whereas by 1974 the rate had increased to 60% for males and 70% for
females, which is still less than the rate for the normally hearing population
(Schein and Delk, 1974). The vast majority of the deaf adults surveyed in
the Altshuler study preferred a deaf spouse (86%), and on the average the
courtship was longer than for a hearing individual. One's attitude toward
one's own deafness was found to be related to preferences about the spouse's
hearing status. Those who denied deafness as a handicap or who were disturbed by their hearing impairment were more prone to desire a hearing
mate. This was particularly true of uneducated deaf women. In actual practice, only 12% to 14% of the deaf population had a normally hearing
spouse. Deaf black persons tended to marry less frequently than white deaf
persons.

As for preference in children, of those wanting children (92%), 6.5%
wanted deaf children, whereas 50% wanted hearing children. The remaining proportion expressed no preference, although it was suggested that this
might have been a *post facto* preference, because many of these persons already had a deaf child.

In terms of family relationships, the educational expectations of deaf
parents for their hearing children were generally found to be higher than for
their deaf children. It was also stated that the deaf parents' attitudes toward
their hearing children were "less sure, apparently bogged down by greater
expectations and an overevaluation of the absence of impaired hearing. Un-
limited potentials are attributed to the hearing child..." (Altshuler, 1963,
p. 122). The deaf children had fewer demands made of them, and the parents had a more realistic understanding of their potential and limitations.

DISCUSSION

In general, the presence of a hearing impairment does seem to have psycho-social consequences, and, in many respects, deafness seems generally to fulfill the requirements of being a defining feature of a subculture. The members of the deaf community are a heterogeneous group, most of whom identify primarily with other members of the group and who have developed their own social and information network that parallels the core culture. It differs from most other subcultures, however, in that most of its members are assimilated into, rather than born into, the subsociety. Additionally, the symbolic expressions of this subsociety are limited, if not virtually nonexistent, with the exception of the existence and use of a different language form, i.e., American Sign Language.

One of the unfortunate side effects of membership within a subculture is the possibility of overt or unconscious stereotyping and prejudice. Such attitudes can and often do have an isolating effect socially and economically. This seems to be the case with deaf people as well. As pointed out, there is evidence to suggest that many deaf people are underemployed. Potential employers seem to be cautious and uncertain about the capabilities of deaf persons and thus underestimate their potential, thereby restricting their employability. It is also true, however, that in many cases this vocational and economic restriction is a function of a lack of vocational information and of an adequate language and academic base.

The fact that ours *is* a pluralistic society and the fact that deaf persons have become more vocal regarding perceived discriminatory practices of normally hearing individuals has given rise to a growing "deaf awareness" and to a militancy that has served to enhance the cohesiveness of at least a portion of this subgroup. It is uncertain, however, how this deaf awareness has worked to the benefit of minority deaf persons, such as black and Spanish-surnamed individuals, who traditionally have been marginal members both of this subgroup and of the core culture.

7

SOME SUMMARY AND CONCLUDING REMARKS

In this concluding chapter we: 1) repeat the two viewpoints stated in the preface, 2) relate the major conclusions of the book's six preceding chapters to those two viewpoints, where possible, and 3) provide a few concluding remarks on the present and possible future directions of the education of deaf children and youth.

Our first viewpoint was that the primary goal of education for typical (non–multiply handicapped) prelingually deaf children should be literacy — the ability to read and write, at a mature level, the general language of society. The second viewpoint was that development of the deaf child's (and, in fact, of any child's) intellectual potential requires an early environment that provides a wealth of stimulating learning experiences that are made meaningful for the child through interaction with other people by means of a fluent and intelligible communication system. Fluent communication is particularly important in infancy and early childhood when the parents or parent surrogates are the principal figures in the child's life.

The two statements are closely related. Reading for hearing people, as we presently understand it, is a secondary or derived language system that is superimposed on the basic internalized auditory language system of hearing children, which, in turn, resulted from fluent oral communication between parent and child in infancy and early childhood. Extensive cognitive experiences and a symbol system (spoken language) with which to internalize and manipulate them are widely recognized as critical for the successful education of hearing children. Similar cognitive experiences and an appropriate symbol system to internalize and manipulate them are probably equally as important for deaf children. The question is, just what is an appropriate symbol system?

It is noted in the first stated viewpoint and elsewhere in the book that our concern has been limited to prelingually deaf children. As defined in Chapter 1, these are children who have sensorineural hearing impairments of at least 90 dB in the better ear and who suffered the impairment prior to the age of 2 to 3 years. We stress again the need for clearly stated definitions or at least descriptions of deaf individuals or groups of individuals. As stated in Chapter 1, much confusion in interpreting educational and research data in the field arises from lack of complete descriptions of the individuals involved and from generalization of findings to dissimilar populations. It is inappropriate to generalize findings obtained with what we would term hard-of-hearing individuals (less than 90 dB) to deaf individuals (greater than 90 dB). It should be recognized that 90 dB is a somewhat arbitrary line. Other authors use varying points on the decibel scale to define "deaf" (for example, 105 dB); the important point is that the sensorineural impairment is of sufficient severity that the individual, even with amplification, must rely on vision as the primary channel for receptive communication. We contend that any impairment of less than about 90 dB is not of sufficient severity to produce such an effect and, therefore, should not be classified as deaf.

In Chapter 2 we conclude that three communication systems seem to have stood the test of time, experience, and research in the education of deaf children — American Sign Language, Pidgin Sign English, and Oral English. It is emphasized, however, that research evidence is scanty, that conclusions at this time must be tentative, and that future research might justify different conclusions. This is particularly true of our conclusion that Pidgin Sign English, used in conjunction with spoken language and good amplification, might be the most promising system for use with the majority of deaf children in infancy and early childhood for communication between parent and child, and that, used in conjunction with an active oral program, such as that proposed by Ling (1976), it might be the most promising system for classroom teaching also. Although Signing Exact English (SEE-II) might be, at present, the system most widely used with deaf children in the classroom (Jordan et al. 1976), there is no evidence that it produces superior results. There is also some evidence that this system and other systems of Manual English evolve in classroom use to non-English systems (Marmor and Pettito, 1979).

The Oral English approach, as typified by the active oral programs of such schools as St. Joseph's School for the Deaf and Central Institute for the Deaf in St. Louis, Missouri; the Clarke School for the Deaf in Northampton, Massachusetts; the Lexington School for the Deaf in New York City; the Tucker-Maxon School in Portland, Oregon; and a number of other residential and day programs, has, in our evaluation of research data, such as that of Corson (1973) and of Ogden (1979), proven of value for at least a significant portion of deaf children. In Chapter 2 we list a number of conditions that seem to be requisites for the success of such programs and conclude that it is difficult for many of those conditions to be met in the general public school programs for deaf children. It is likely, however, that many more children could benefit from active oral programs than is presently the case. It should be possible to provide those parents who want this educational option for their deaf children with the financial support and programs to make it feasible.

As we state in Chapter 2, American Sign Language is probably the system of choice for communication among a majority of deaf people in the United States, regardless of how they were educated. It is their language and their preferred means of communication and should be encouraged to flourish and to evolve just as any linguistically natural language. It is, however, the *first language* probably only for those deaf children who have deaf parents. That raises the significant question of whether it should be actively promoted as the first language and communication system of deaf children of hearing parents and, if so, just how that can be practically managed. The promotion of ASL as the first language for *all* deaf children might well be the great issue of the 1980s, as Total Communication was of the 1970s (and still is), Cued Speech of the late 1960s, and Neo-Oralism (the Rochester Method, fingerspelling and speech) of the 1950s and early 1960s.

The issue of communication systems, which are detailed and discussed in Chapter 2, has in the past been strongly linked to the types of educational programs available for deaf children as discussed in Chapter 3. Until the 1970s, day programs were almost exclusively oral, and residential schools (with the exception of the oral, mostly private, ones) used manual communication at least in the upper grades and permitted its use in out-of-class situations. With Total Communication as a rallying cry and the limited results of oralism as practiced in most day programs as justification, a movement began that resulted in the addition of manual communication to many public day programs, so that presently systems of communication no longer differentiate between day and residential programs. There might, however, still be differences between the two types of programs in the particular type of manual system used, with day programs being more likely to use some form of SEE-II and residential schools using some form of Pidgin Sign English.

The shift of deaf student enrollment from residential schools to day programs has continued unabated for decades. In addition, increasing numbers of deaf children are attending residential schools as day students. At present, the enrollment nationally is about 70% day students and 30% residential students, with considerable variation from state to state, depending upon the number and concentration or dispersion of deaf children. Although one would hope that the shift would affect positively our criterion of literacy stated in the preface, there is no evidence that it has done so for what we have defined as deaf students. Both Quigley and Frisina (1961) and Karchmer and Peterson (1980) found that day students in residential schools differed significantly from resident students in the same schools, primarily only on speech intelligibility.

Mainstreaming seems to be a logical extension of the shift to day programs in the education of deaf children, and it might seem that we have slighted its importance as a major movement in special education for all types of disabled children. As we pointed out in Chapter 3, however, mainstreaming has been tried extensively in the past with deaf children. Also, we tend to agree with Kirk, as cited in Moores (1978), that many of the successes claimed for the mainstreaming of retarded and other types of disabled children involve children who never should have been in special programs in the first place. Mainstreaming will continue. It is a significant social movement with many obvious positive features, one of those being the value of exposing children in the general school population to disabled children as a part of, rather than apart from, the general society.

Although we recognize and support the positive aspects of mainstreaming, we caution that its merits should not be overstated, as is often the case with such movements (Total Communication is another case in point). In Chapter 3, we present most of the *data-based* publications we could find on the matter. Two important points stand out in those studies. First, apparently only a very small number of what we have defined as *deaf* children are being fully mainstreamed. Probably many more *hard-of-hearing* children are receiving this treatment and are being perceived as being deaf. Second, the data do not indicate improvements in literacy, which we state in the preface and at the beginning of this chapter as our primary criterion of educational success. A number of schools, such as St. Joseph's School for the Deaf, Clarke School for the Deaf, and others, have had, for as long as a century, the goal of placing their deaf students in the regular schools as soon as possible. Even with their many advantages and outstanding programs, those schools have found the task extremely difficult. Their experience would argue that the mainstreaming of deaf children in the public schools with limited (or even extensive) support services should be approached with caution.

In Chapter 3, we present some information concerning various types of regional programs for deaf children and conclude that these might be the popular programs of the next decade for deaf children. A few cautions: first, there are no data showing significant effects of the programs on our defining criterion of literacy. Second, the programs require a degree of voluntary co-operation among local school systems that is often difficult to obtain and maintain. Third, the diversity of approaches to all aspects of education that is typical of American education argues against any type of program becoming the prevailing one. Most likely, and depending upon local conditions and attitudes, all of the types of programs described — residential schools, day programs, day classes, regional programs, and mainstreaming — will find a place. A concluding note on this issue of type of educational placement is that, in Illinois and, we understand, in other states, groups are promoting legislation that would allow the parents of a deaf child to select whether their child should attend local day or mainstreamed programs or the state residential school. If any of these legislative attempts is successful, it will add another interesting option to an already interesting variety.

The evidence presented in Chapter 4 indicates that differences still are found on various cognitive tasks between deaf and hearing individuals that cannot at present be accounted for other than by assuming that they are a result of deafness. Most recent studies indicate, however, that there are not important differences between deaf and hearing people on *general* intellectual ability, and most researchers and educators of deaf children presently seem to accept that differences that do exist on specific cognitive tasks between deaf and hearing persons are not significant for educational achievement. It follows that the inability of deaf children to meet the criterion of literacy, which we stated should be the determining criterion of educational success, is not because of inherent disabilities in the children, but because of disabilities in the educational system. We simply do not yet know how to realize fully the educational potential of deaf children, although a thousand different voices might disagree and protest in favor of their particular approaches.

We consider Chapter 5 to be the educational heart of our book. It deals with reading and written language, and we state in the preface and again at the beginning of this chapter that the ability to read and write the general language of society at a mature level is our primary criterion for educational success with deaf children. As the data clearly show, however, few deaf children attain this criterion. Study after study cited in Chapter 5 shows that many deaf students never reach the level of functional literacy (fourth-grade reading level), have similarly low levels of written language performance, and usually have overall academic achievements lower than sixth-grade level at school-leaving age. The low reading achievement levels are accompanied by even lower levels of performance when specific aspects of reading are investigated. Vocabulary, syntax, and inferential abilities all show deficiencies. We believe that much of this reading deficiency is because of the lack in most deaf children of a well-developed, internalized language system on which reading can be superimposed. The development of such an internalized language system depends, as we state in the preface, on a wealth of early cognitive experiences that the child can internalize and manipulate by means of a symbol system that has developed through some means of fluent communication established with parents and others in the early environment. The key seems to be the early development of a fluent symbol system, which raises the hoary question of what form that symbol system should take. We are back again to considering what forms of language and communication we should encourage as the deaf child's first language system.

In Chapter 6 we show that deafness seems to fulfill the requirements of being a defining feature of a subculture. The members of a deaf community are a heterogeneous group, who identify primarily with other members of the group and who have developed their own social and information network that parallels the general culture. This subculture differs in at least one significant respect from most other subcultures—most of its members are assimilated into it rather than born into it. Only deaf children of deaf parents (and not even all of them) can be considered to be truly born into the culture. Most of the members are assimilated into the subculture by one great binding common factor—the American Sign Language. This brings us again, as almost every chapter in the book does, to the issue of language and communication.

Most issues in the education of deaf children reduce to this dual issue of language and communication. In spite of efforts to resolve the problem beginning with the initial controversies of Heinicke and de l'Épée in about 1780, continuing with the declaration in favor or oralism at the Conference of Milan in 1880, and more recently appearing in the attempts of Total Communication to declare it a nonissue in 1980, the issue of language and communication remains central in the education of deaf children and will remain so until sufficient appropriate research data have been collected to provide some resolution of it. It is possible that considerable progress toward resolving the issue (if, indeed, it is resolvable) will be made in the next decade or two. The growth of education and of social and behavioral research during the past 20 years has laid the groundwork for progress and has brought forth a substantial number of linguists, psycholinguists, cognitive psychologists, and other types of social and behavioral scientists interested in deafness and deaf people. Many of those researchers are now exploring such areas as cochlear implants to replace the damaged or destroyed inner ear mechanism of hearing; the structure, function, and use of ASL; the effectiveness of various communication systems, such as Cued Speech, Pidgin Sign English, and Signing Exact English; various devices for converting the acoustic signals of speech into visual codes that can be read rather than heard; the interaction of deaf children with their parents and others in infancy and very early childhood; and a host of other topics that could promise significant progress for the education of deaf children.

Perhaps one of the most positive features of the interest in deafness by a variety of social and behavioral scientists is that the study of deaf people is increasingly seen as a part of the study of people in general rather than of a unique population. Linguists view ASL as a language with features similar to other languages, psycholinguists see language development of deaf children as part of all child language development, and so forth. This joining of research on various aspects of deaf children to social and behavioral research in general should have mutual benefits: the education of deaf children should benefit, and basic research on child language and development should benefit. Applied research should be another beneficiary. Quigley and King (1981a) have shown that almost all of the error patterns of deaf students on various tests of English structure are also found in individuals from various first language backgrounds who are learning English as a second language. In the near future there will probably be a variety of attempts to use the techniques of bilingual teaching and of English as a second language with deaf students.

REFERENCES

Allen, D. 1971. Modality of similarity and hearing ability. Psychonom. Sci. 24:69–71.

Alpern, G., and Boll, T. 1972. Alpern-Boll Developmental Profile. Psychological Development Publications, Indianapolis, Indiana.

Altshuler, K. 1963. Sexual patterns and family relationships. In: J. Rainer, K. Altshuler, and F. Kallmann (eds.), Family and Mental Health Problems in a Deaf Population. New York State Psychiatric Institute, New York.

Altshuler, K., and Baroff, G. 1963. Educational background and vocational adjustment. In: J. Rainer, K. Altshuler, and F. Kallman (eds.), Family and Mental Health Problems in a Deaf Population. New York State Psychiatric Institute, New York.

Altshuler, K., Deming, W., Vollenweider, J., Rainer, J., and Tendler, R. 1976. Impulsivity and profound early deafness: A cross cultural inquiry. Am. Ann. Deaf 121:331–345.

American National Standards Institute. 1969. American National Standard Specifications for Audiometers (ANSI S3.6–1969). American National Standards Institute, New York.

Anthony, D. 1966. Seeing essential English. Unpublished master's thesis, Eastern Michigan University, Ypsilanti, Michigan.

Babb, R. 1979. A study of the academic achievement and language acquisition levels of deaf children of hearing parents in an educational environment using Signing Exact English as the primary mode of communication. Unpublished doctoral dissertation, University of Illinois, Urbana.

Babbini, B., and Quigley, S. 1970. A Study of the Growth Patterns in Language, Communication, and Educational Achievement in Six Residential Schools for Deaf Students. Institute for Research on Exceptional Children, Urbana, Illinois.

Bachara, G., Raphael, J., and Phelan, W. 1980. Empathy development in deaf preadolescents. Am. Ann. Deaf 125:38–41.

Baddeley, A. 1979. Working memory and reading. In: P. Kolers and M. Wrolstad (eds.), Processing of Visible Language, Vol. 1. Plenum Press, New York.

Badger, E. 1971. Teaching Guide: Infant Learning Program. Instructo Corporations, Paoli, Pennsylvania.

Baroff, G. 1963. Patterns of socialization and community integration. In: J. Rainer, K. Altshuler, and F. Kallman (eds.), Family and Mental Health Problems in a Deaf Population. New York State Psychiatric Institute, New York.

Baron, J. 1973. Phonemic stage not necessary for reading. Quart. J. of Exper. Psychol. 25:241–246.

Bates, E. 1979. The Emergence of Symbols: Cognition and Communication in Infancy. Academic Press, New York.

Beaver, J. 1968. Transformational grammar and the teaching of reading. Res. Teach. English 2:161–171.

Bellugi, U., Klima, E., and Siple, P. 1974. Remembering in signs. Cognition 3:93–125.

Belmont, J., Karchmer, M., and Pilkonis, P. 1976. Instructed rehearsal strategies influence on deaf memory processing. J. Speech Hear. Res. 19:36–47.

Belmont, J., and Karchmer, M. 1978. Deaf people's memory: There are problems testing special problems. In: M. Gruneberg, P. Morris, and R. Sykes (eds.), Practical Aspects of Memory. Academic Press, London.

Bender, R. 1960. The Conquest of Deafness. The Press of Western Reserve University, Cleveland, Ohio.

Best, B., and Roberts, G. 1976. Early cognitive development in hearing impaired children. Am. Ann. Deaf 121:560–564.

Best, H. 1943. Deafness and the Deaf in the United States. Macmillan Publishing Company, Inc., New York.

Birch, J. 1975. Hearing Impaired Children in the Mainstream. Council for Exceptional Children, Reston, Virginia.

Blanton, R., Nunnally, J., and Odom, P. 1967. Graphemic, phonetic, and associative factors in the verbal behavior of deaf and hearing subjects. J. Speech Hear. Res. 10:225–231.

Bloom, L., and Lahey, M. 1978. Language Development and Language Disorders. John Wiley & Sons, Inc., New York.

Bonet, J. 1620. Reducion de las letras y arte para ensenar a hablar los mudos. Par Francisco Arbaco de Angelo, Madrid.

Bornstein, H. 1973. A description of some current sign systems designed to represent English. Am. Ann. Deaf 118:454–463.

Bornstein, H., Saulnier, K., and Hamilton, L. 1980. Signed English: A first evaluation. Am. Ann. Deaf 125:467–481.

Bowlby, J. 1954. Maternal Care and Mental Health. World Health Organization, Geneva.

Bragg, B. 1973. Ameslish—Our American heritage: A testimony. Am. Ann. Deaf 118:672–674.

Brasel, K., and Quigley, S. 1977. The influence of certain language and communication environments in early childhood on the development of language in deaf individuals. J. Speech Hear. Res. 20:95–107.

Brill, R. 1969. The superior IQs of deaf children of deaf parents. California Palms 15:1–4.

Brill, R. 1978. Mainstreaming the Prelingually Deaf Child. Gallaudet College Press, Washington, D.C.

Brimer, A. 1972. Wide-span Reading Test. Thomas Nelson and Sons, Ltd., London.

Caccamise, F., and Drury, A. 1976. A review of current terminology in education of the deaf. Deaf American 29:7–10.

Carnine, D., and Silbert, J. 1979. Direct Instruction Reading. Charles E. Merrill Pub. Co., Columbus, Ohio.

Carrow, E. 1974. A test using elicited imitation in assessing grammatical structure in children. J. Speech Hear. Dis. 39:437–444.

Chall, J. 1967. Learning to Read: The Great Debate. McGraw-Hill Book Company, New York.

Chen, K. 1976. Acoustic image in visual detection for deaf and hearing college students. J. Gen. Psychol. 94:243–246.

Chomsky, N. 1957. Syntactic Structures. Mouton, The Hague.

Chomsky, N. 1965. Aspects of the Theory of Syntax. MIT Press, Cambridge, Massachusetts.

Chomsky, N. 1976. Reflections on Language. Temple-Smith, London.

Clarke, A., and Clarke, A. 1977. Early Experiences: Myth and Evidence. Free Press, New York.

Clarke, B., and Ling, D. 1976. The effects of using cued speech: A follow-up study. Volta Rev. 78:23–34.

Cohen, G. 1977. The Psychology of Cognition. Academic Press, London.

Collins, J. 1969. Communication between deaf children of preschool age and their mothers. Unpublished doctoral dissertation, University of Pittsburgh, Pennsylvania.

Collins-Ahlgren, M. 1975. Language development of two deaf children. Am. Ann. Deaf 120:524–539.

Conlin, D., and Paivio, A. 1975. The associative learning of the deaf, the effects of word imagery and sign ability. Mem. Cognition 3:335–340.

Conrad, R. 1970. Short-term memory processes in the deaf. Bri. J. Psychol. 61:179–195.

Conrad, R. 1971. The effect of vocalizing on comprehension in the profoundly deaf. Br. J. Psychol. 62:147–150.

Conrad, R. 1979. The Deaf School Child. Harper and Row, London.

Conrad, R., and Rush, M. 1965. On the nature of short-term memory encoding by the deaf. J. Speech Hear. Dis. 30:336–343.

Cooper, R., and Rosenstein, J. 1966. Language acquisition of deaf children. Volta Rev. 68:58–67.

Cornett, O. 1967. Cued speech. Am. Ann. Deaf, 112:3–13.

Corson, H. 1973. Comparing deaf children of oral parents and deaf parents using manual communication with deaf children of hearing parents on academic, social, and communication functioning. Unpublished doctoral dissertation, University of Cincinnati, Ohio.

Craig, W., Salem, J., and Craig, H. 1976. Mainstreaming and partial integration of deaf with hearing students. Am. Ann. Deaf 121:63–68.

Cromer, R. 1976. The cognitive hypothesis of language acquisition and its implications for child language deficiency. In: D. Morehead and A. Morehead (eds.), Normal and Deficient Child Language. University Park Press, Baltimore.

Dale, P. 1976. Language Development: Structure and Function. Holt, Rinehart, & Winston, Inc., New York.

Davis, H., and Silverman, R. 1978. Hearing and Deafness, 3rd Ed. Holt, Rinehart, & Winston, Inc., New York.

Demerath, N., and Maxwell, G. 1976. Sociology: Perspectives and Applications. Harper and Row Publishers, New York.

Dennis, W. 1960. Causes of retardation among institutional children: Iran. J. Gen. Psychol. 96:47–59.

Denton, D. 1970. Remarks in support of a system of total communication for deaf children. In: Communication Symposium, Maryland School for the Deaf, Frederick, Maryland.

de Villiers, J., and de Villiers, P. 1978. Language Acquisition. Harvard University Press, Cambridge, Massachusetts.

DiFrancesca, S. 1972. Academic Achievement Test Results of a National Testing Program for Hearing Impaired Students, United States, Spring, 1971, Series D, no. 9. Gallaudet College, Office of Demographic Studies, Washington, D.C.

Doehring, D., Bonnycastle, D., and Ling, A. 1978. Rapid reading skills of integrated hearing-impaired children. Volta Rev. 80:399–409.

Doll, E. 1953. The Measurement of Social Competence. Educational Test Bureau, Minneapolis, Minnesota.

Eriksen, C., Pollack, M., and Montague, W. 1970. Implicit speech: Mechanism in perceptual encoding? J. Exper. Psych. 84:502–507.

Evans, A. 1975. Experiential deprivation: Unresolved factor in the impoverished socialization of deaf school children in residence. Am. Ann. Deaf 120:545–552.

Evans, L. 1966. A comparative study of the Wechsler Intelligence Scale for Children (Performance) and the Raven's Progressive Matrices with deaf children. Teacher of the Deaf 64:76–82.

Farrugia, D., and Austin, G. 1980. A study of socio-emotional adjustment patterns of hearing-impaired students in different educational settings. Am. Ann. Deaf 125:535–541.

Federation Employment and Guidance Service. 1959. Survey of Employers' Practices and Policies in Hiring of the Physically Impaired Worker. Federal Employment and Guidance Commission, New York.

Fitz-Gerald, D., and Fitz-Gerald, M. 1976. Sex education survey of residential facilities for the deaf. Am. Ann. Deaf 121:480–483.

Friedman, L. (Ed.). 1977. On the Other Hand. Academic Press, New York.

Frumkin, B., and Anisfeld, M. 1977. Semantic and surface codes in the memory of deaf children. Cog. Psychol. 9:475–493.

Furfey, P., and Harte, T. 1968. Interaction of Deaf and Hearing in Baltimore City, Maryland. Catholic University of America, Washington, D.C.

Furth, H. 1964. Conservation of weight in deaf and hearing children. Child. Dev. 35:143–150.

Furth, H. 1966a. Thinking without Language: Psychological Implications of Deafness. Free Press, New York.

Furth, H. 1966b. A comparison of reading test norms of deaf and hearing children. Am. Ann. Deaf 111:461–462.

Furth, H. 1970. A review and perspective on the thinking of deaf people. In: J. Hellmuth (ed.), Cognitive Studies: Vol. 1. Brunner/Mazel Publisher, New York.

Furth, H. 1973. Deafness and Learning: A Psychosocial Approach. Wadsworth Publishing Company, Inc., Belmont, California.

Furth, H., and Youniss, J. 1965. The influence of language and experience on discovery and use of logical symbols. Br. J. Psychol. 56:381–390.

Furth, H., and Youniss, J. 1971. Formal operations and language: A comparison of deaf and hearing adolescents. Int. J. Psychol. 6:49–64.

Fusfeld, I. 1955. The academic program of schools for the deaf. Volta Rev. 57:63–70.

Garrison, W., and Tesch, S. 1978. Self concept and deafness: A review of research literature. Volta Rev. 80:457–466.

Geers, A., and Moog, J. 1978. Syntactic maturity of spontaneous speech and elicited imitations of hearing-impaired children. J. Speech Hear. Dis. 43:380–391.

Gentile, A., and McCarthy, B. 1973. Additional Handicapping Conditions among Hearing Impaired Students, United States: 1971–72, Series, D, no. 14. Office of Demographic Studies, Gallaudet College, Washington, D.C.

Goetzinger, C., and Rousey, C. 1959. Educational achievement of deaf children. Am. Ann. Deaf 104:221–231.

Goldenberg, M., Rabinowitz, A., and Kravetz, S. 1979. The relation between communication levels and self-concept of deaf parents and their normal children. Am. Ann. Deaf 124:472–478.

Gordon, M. 1970. The subsociety and the subculture. In: D. Arnold (ed.), The Sociology of Subcultures. The Glendessary Press, Berkely, California.

Goss, R. 1970. Language used by mothers of deaf children and mothers of hearing children. Am. Ann. Deaf 115:93–96.

Graham, E., and Shapiro, E. 1953. Use of the performance scale of the WISC with the deaf child. J. Consult. Psychol. 17:396–398.

Green, D., and Shallice, T. 1976. Direct visual access in reading for meaning. Mem. Cognition 41:753–758.

Greenberg, M. 1980a. Hearing families with deaf children: Stress and functioning as related to communication method. Am. Ann. Deaf 125:1063–1071.

Greenberg, M. 1980b. Social interactions between deaf preschoolers and their mothers: The effects of communication method and communication competence. Dev. Psychol. 16:465–474.

Greenberg, M., and Marvin, R. 1979. Attachment patterns in profoundly deaf preschool children. Merrill-Palmer Q. 25:265–279.

Greenstein, J., Greenstein, B., McConville, K., and Stellini, L. 1975. Mother-infant Communication and Language Acquisition in Deaf Infants. Lexington School for the Deaf, New York.

Gustason, G., Pfetzing, D., and Zawolkow, E. 1975. Signing Exact English, Rev. Ed. Modern Signs Press, Rossmor, California.

Hall, M., and Ramig, C. 1978. Linguistics Foundation for Reading. Charles E. Merrill Publishing Company, Columbus, Ohio.

Hammermeister, F. 1971. Reading achievement in deaf adults. Am. Ann. Deaf 116:25–28.

Hardyck, C., and Petrinovich, L. 1970. Subvocal speech and comprehension level as a function of the difficulty level of reading material. J. Verb. Learn. Behav. 9:647–652.

Harris, R. 1978. The relationship of impulse control to parent hearing status, manual communication, and academic achievement in deaf children. Am. Ann. Deaf 123:52–67.

Harvey, V., and Luongo, E. 1945. Physical impairment and job performance. JAMA 127:902–907, 961–970.

Hatcher, C., and Robbins, N. 1978. The development of reading skills in hearing-impaired children. Paper presented at the Annual Meeting of the National Reading Conference, November 30–December 2, St. Petersburg Beach, Florida.

Heider, F. 1972. Universals in color naming and memory. J. Exper. Psychol. 93:511–512.

Heider, F., and Heider, G. 1940. A Comparison of Sentence Structure of Deaf and Hearing Children. Psychol. Monographs 52:54–103.

Hess, W. 1960. Personality adjustment in deaf children. Unpublished doctoral dissertation. University of Rochester, New York.

Hunt, J., Mohandessi, K., Ghodssi, M., and Akiyama, M. 1976. The Psychological Development of Orphanage-Reared Infants: Interventions with Outcomes (Tehran). Genet. Psychol. Monograph 94:117–226.

Jarvella, R. 1971. Syntactic processing of connected speech. J. Verb. Learn. Verb. Behav. 10:409–416.

Jarvella, R. 1979. Immediate memory and discourse processing. In: G. Bower (ed.), The Psychology of Learning and Motivation. Academic Press, New York.

Jennings, H. 1951. Twice handicapped. Occup. Psychol. 30:176–181.

Jensema, C., and Trybus, R. 1978. Communication Patterns and Educational Achievement of Hearing Impaired Students, Series T, no. 2. Gallaudet College, Office of Demographic Studies, Washington, D.C.

Joiner, L., Erickson, E., and Crittenden, J. 1968. Occupational plans and aspirations of deaf adolescents. J. Rehab. Deaf 2:20–26.

Joiner, L., Erickson, E., Crittenden, J., and Stevenson, V. 1969. Predicting the academic achievement of the acoustically-impaired using intelligence and self-concept of academic ability. J. Spec. Ed. 3:425–431.

Jordan, I., Gustason, G., and Rosen, R., 1976. Current communication trends in programs for the deaf. Am. Ann. Deaf 121:527–532.

Karchmer, M., and Petersen, L. 1980. Commuter Students at Residential Schools for the Deaf. Office of Demographic Studies, Gallaudet College, Washington, D.C.

Karchmer, M., and Trybus, R. 1977. Who are the Deaf Children in "Mainstream" Programs? Series R, no. 4. Office of Demographic Studies, Gallaudet College, Washington, D.C.

Kavanagh, J. (ed.). 1968. Communicating by Language: The Reading Process. U.S. Department of Health, Education, and Welfare, Bethesda, Maryland.

Kavanagh, J., and Mattingly, I. (eds.). 1972. Language by Ear and by Eye: The Relationship between Speech and Reading. MIT Press, Cambridge, Massachusetts.

Kelly, R., and Tomlinson-Keasey, C. 1976. Information-processing of visually presented pictures and word stimuli by young hearing impaired and normally hearing children. J. Speech Hear. Res. 19:628–638.

Klaber, M., and Falek, A. 1963. Delinquency and crime. In: J. Rainer, K. Altshuler, and F. Kallmann (eds.), Family and Mental Health Problems in a Deaf Population. New York State Psychiatric Institute, New York.

Klapp, S. 1972. Implicit speech inferred from response latencies in same-different decisions. In: J. Kavanagh and I. Mattingly (eds.), Language by Ear and by Eye: The Relationship between Speech and Reading. MIT Press, Cambridge, Massachusetts.

Kleiman, G. 1975. Speech recoding in reading. J. Verb. Learn. Verb. Behav. 14:323–339.

Klima, E., and Bellugi, U. 1979. The Signs of Language. Harvard University Press, Cambridge, Massachusetts.

Kretschmer, R., and Kretschmer, L. 1978. Language Development and Intervention with the Hearing Impaired. University Park Press, Baltimore.

Lake, D. 1978. Syntax and sequential memory in hearing impaired children. In: H. Reynolds and C. Williams (eds.), Proceedings of the Gallaudet Conference on Reading in Relation to Deafness. Gallaudet College, Washington, D.C.

Lane, H., and Baker, D. 1974. Reading achievement of the deaf: Another look. Volta Rev. 76:489–499.

Lane, H., and Grosjean, F. 1980. Recent Perspectives on American Sign Language. Lawrence Erlbaum Associates, Hillsdale, New Jersey.

LaSasso, C. 1978. National survey of materials and procedures used to teach reading to hearing-impaired children. Am. Ann. Deaf 123:22–30.

Lee, L. 1974. Developmental Sentence Analysis. Northwestern University Press, Evanston, Illinois.

Lerman, A., and Guilfoyle, G. 1970. The Development of Pre-Vocational Behavior in Deaf Adolescents. Teachers College Press, New York.

Levine, E. 1956. Youth in a Silent World. New York University Press, New York.

Levine, E. 1976. Psycho-cultural determinants in personality development. Volta Rev. 78:258-267.

Levine, E., and Wagner, E. 1974. Personality patterns of deaf persons: An interpretation based on research with the Hands Test. Percep. Motor Skills 39:1167-1236.

Levy, B. 1978. Speech analysis during sentence processing: Reading and listening. Visible Lang. 12:81-102.

Lichtenstein, E. 1980. A Proposal for the Experimental Investigation of Recording Strategies Used by Deaf Readers during Reading Comprehension. Center for the Study of Reading, University of Illinois, Urbana.

Ling, D. 1976. Speech and the Hearing Impaired Child: Theory and Practice. A. G. Bell Association for the Deaf, Inc., Washington, D.C.

Ling, D., and Clarke, B. 1975. Cued speech: An evaluative study. Am. Ann. Deaf 120:480-488.

Ling, D., and Ling, A. 1978. Aural Habilitation: The Foundations of Verbal Learning in Hearing-impaired Children. A. G. Bell Association for the Deaf, Inc., Washington, D.C.

Locke, J. 1978. Phonemic effects in the silent reading of hearing and deaf children. Cognition 6:175-187.

Locke, J., and Locke, V. 1971. Deaf children's phonetic, visual, and dactylic coding in a grapheme recall task. J. Exper. Psychol. 89:142-146.

Lunde, A., and Bigman, S. 1959. Occupational Conditions among the Deaf. Gallaudet College, Washington, D.C.

MacDonald, A. 1973. Internal-external locus of control. In: J. Robinson and P. Shaver (eds.), Measures of Social Psychological Attitudes. Institute for Social Research, Ann Arbor, Michigan.

MacNamara, J. 1977. On the relationship between language learning and thought. In: J. MacNamara (ed.), Language Learning and Thought. Academic Press, New York.

McAndrews, H. 1948. Rigidity and isolation: A study of the deaf and blind. J. Abnorm. Soc. Psychol. 43:467-494.

McCrone, W. 1979. Learned helplessness and level of underachievement among deaf adolescents. Psychol. Schools 16:430-434.

McGee, D. 1976. Mainstreaming problems and procedures: Age 6-12. In: G. Nix (ed.), Mainstream Education for Hearing Impaired Children and Youth. Grune & Stratton, New York.

McGuigan, F. 1970. Covert oral behavior during the silent performance of language tasks. Psychol. Bull. 74:309-326.

McKee, P., Harrison, M., McCowen, A., Lehr, E., and Durr, W. 1966. Reading for Meaning, 4th Ed. Houghton Mifflin Company, Boston.

McKeever, W., Hoemann, H., Florian, V., and Van Deventer, A. 1976. Evidence of minimal cerebral asymmetries for the processing of English words and American Sign Language in the congenitally deaf. Neuropsychologia 14:413-423.

McLaughlin, J., and Andrews, J. 1975. The reading habits of deaf adults in Baltimore. Am. Ann. Deaf 120:497-501.

McNeil, D. 1978. Speech and thought. In: I. Markova (ed.), The Social Context of Language. John Wiley & Sons, New York.

Magner, M. 1964. Reading: Goals and achievements at Clarke School for the Deaf. Volta Rev. 66:464-468.

Manning, A., Goble, W., Markman, R., and LaBreche, T. 1977. Lateral cerebral differences in the deaf in response to linguistic and nonlinguistic stimuli. Brain Lang. 4:309–321.

Marmor, G., and Pettito, L. 1979. Simultaneous Communication in the Classroom: How Well is English Grammar Represented. Department of Human Development and Family Studies, Cornell University, Ithaca, New York.

Marshall, W., and Quigley, S. 1970. Quantitative and Qualitative Analysis of Syntactic Structure in the Written Language of Deaf Students. Institute for Research on Exceptional Children, University of Illinois, Urbana.

Meadow, K. 1967. The effect of early manual communication and family climate on the deaf child's development. Unpublished doctoral dissertation, University of California, Berkeley.

Meadow, K. 1976. The development of deaf children. In: E. Hetherington (ed.), Review of Child Development Research, Vol. 5. University of Chicago Press, Chicago.

Meadow, K., and Trybus, R. 1979. Behavioral and emotional problems of deaf children: An overview. In: L. Bradford and W. Hardy (eds.), Hearing and Hearing Impairment. Grune & Stratton, New York.

Mills v. Board of Education of District of Columbia. 1972. 348 F. Supp. 866, 968, 875 (DDC).

Moores, D. 1967. Applications of "cloze" procedures to the assessment of psycholinguistic abilities of the deaf. Unpublished doctoral dissertation, University of Illinois, Urbana.

Moores, D. 1978. Educating the Deaf: Psychology, Principles, and Practices. Houghton Mifflin Company, Boston.

Moores, D. 1979. Model post secondary vocational-technical programs for the deaf: Attitudes of staff and students. J. Rehabil. Deaf 12:15–23.

Morkovin, B. 1960. Experiment in teaching deaf preschool children in the Soviet Union. Volta Rev. 62:260–268.

Moulton, R., and Beasley, D. 1975. Verbal coding strategies used by hearing-impaired individuals. J. Speech Hear. Res. 18:559–570.

Myklebust, H. 1960. The Psychology of Deafness. Grune & Stratton, New York.

Neville, H., and Bellugi, U. 1978. Patterns of cerebral specialization in congenitally deaf adults: A preliminary report. In: P. Siple (ed.), Understanding Language through Sign Language Research. Academic Press, New York.

Neyhus, A. 1964. The social and emotional adjustment of deaf adults. Volta Rev. 66: 319–325.

Nicholls, G. 1979. Cued speech and the reception of spoken language. Unpublished master's thesis. McGill University, Montreal, Canada.

Nix, G. 1976. Mainstream Education for Hearing Impaired Children and Youth. Grune & Stratton, New York.

Northcott, W. 1973. The Hearing Impaired Child in a Regular Classroom: Preschool, Elementary, and Secondary Years. A. G. Bell Association, Washington, D.C.

O'Conner, N., and Hermelin, B. 1978. Seeing and Hearing and Space and Time. Academic Press, New York.

Odom, P., Blanton, R., and McIntyre, C. 1970. Coding medium and word recall by deaf and hearing subjects. J. Speech Hear. Res. 13:54–58.

Office of Demographic Studies. 1972. Academic Achievement Test Results of a National Testing Program for Hearing Impaired Students. Gallaudet College, Washington, D.C.

Ogden, P. 1979. Experiences and attitudes of oral deaf adults regarding oralism. Unpublished doctoral dissertation, University of Illinois, Urbana.

Oleron, P. 1953. Conceptual thinking of the deaf. Am. Ann. Deaf 98:304–310.

O'Neill, M. 1973. The receptive language competence of deaf children in the use of the base structure rules of transformational generative grammar. Unpublished doctoral dissertation, University of Pittsburgh, Pennsylvania.

Ottem, E. 1980. An analysis of cognitive studies with deaf subjects. Am. Ann. Deaf 125:564–575.

Pennsylvania Association for Retarded Citizens (PARC) v. *Commonwealth of Pennsylvania*, 1971, 1972. 334 F. Supp. 1256 (E.D. Pa.), 343 F. Supp. 279, 282, 296 (E.D. Pa.).

Pflaster, G. 1980. A factor analysis of variables related to academic performance of hearing impaired children in regular classes. Volta Rev. 82:71–84.

Phillips, G. 1975a. An exploration of employer attitudes concerning employment opportunities for deaf people. J. Rehabil. Deaf 9:1–9.

Phillips, G. 1975b. Specific jobs for deaf workers identified by employers. J. Rehabil. Deaf 9:10–23.

Phippard, D. 1977. Hemifield differences in visual perception in deaf and hearing subjects. Neuropsychologia 15:555–561.

Pino, J. 1970. Employer ratings of the suitability of certain occupations for deaf persons and the vocational status of deaf employees in certain industries. Unpublished doctoral dissertation, University of Illinois, Urbana.

Pintner, R., and Patterson, D. 1916. A measurement of the language ability of deaf children. Psychol. Rev. 23:413–436.

Pintner, R., and Reamer, J. 1920. A mental and educational survey of schools for the deaf. Am. Ann. Deaf 65:277–300.

Pintner, R., Eisenson, J., and Stanton, M. 1941. The Psychology of the Physically Handicapped. Crofts and Co., New York.

Poizner, H., and Lane, H. 1979. Cerebral asymmetry in the perception of American Sign Language. Brain Lang. 7:210–226.

Poizner, H., Battison, R., and Lane, H. 1979. Cerebral asymmetry for American Sign Language: The effects of moving stimuli. Brain Lang. 7:351–362.

Power, D., and Quigley, S. 1973. Deaf children's acquisition of the passive voice. J. Speech Hear. Res. 16:5–11.

Pressnell, L. 1973. Hearing-impaired children's comprehension and production of syntax in oral language. J. Speech Hear. Res. 16:12–21.

Public Law 94–142. 1975. Education for All Handicapped Children Act of 1975 (S.6). 94th Congress: 1st Session.

Pugh, G. 1946. Summaries from appraisal of the silent reading abilities of acoustically handicapped children. Am. Ann. Deaf 91:331–349.

Quarrington, B., and Solomon, B. 1975. A current study of the social maturity of deaf students. Canadian J. Behav. Sci./Rev. Canadian Sci. Comp. 7:70–77.

Quigley, S. 1969. The Influence of Fingerspelling on the Development of Language, Communication, and Educational Achievement in Deaf Children. Institute for Research on Exceptional Children, Urbana, Illinois.

Quigley, S., and Frisina, D. 1961. Institutionalization and Psychoeducational Development of Deaf Children. CEC Research Monograph, Urbana, Illinois.

Quigley, S., and King, C. 1981a. An invited article: Syntactic performance of hearing impaired and normal hearing individuals. Appl. Psycholinguist. 1:329–356.

Quigley, S., and King, C. 1981b. Reading Milestones, Teacher's Guide, Levels 1, 2, 3. Dormac, Inc., Beaverton, Oregon.

Quigley, S., and King, C. In press. Language development of deaf children and youth. In: S. Rosenberg (ed.), Handbook of Applied Psycholinguistics. Lawrence Erlbaum Associates, New Jersey.

Quigley, S., Jenne, W., and Phillips, S. 1969. Deaf Students in Colleges and Universities. A. G. Bell Association, Washington, D.C.

Quigley, S., Montanelli, D., and Wilbur, R. 1976. Some aspects of the verb system in the language of deaf students. J. Speech Hear. Res. 19:536–550.

Quigley, S., Power, D., and Steinkamp, M. 1977. The language structure of deaf children. Volta Rev. 79:73–84.

Quigley, S., Smith, N., and Wilbur, R. 1974. Comprehension of relativized sentences by deaf students. J. Speech Hear. Res. 17:325–341.

Quigley, S., Wilbur, R., and Montanelli, D. 1974. Question formation in the language of deaf students. J. Speech Hear. Res. 17:699–713.

Quigley, S., Wilbur, R., and Montanelli, D. 1976. Complement structures in the language of deaf students. J. Speech Hear. Res. 19:448–457.

Quigley, S., Jones, B., Erbe, B., and Ferber, R. 1975. An Evaluation of the Regional Programs for Educating Low-incidence Disabled Children in Illinois. Survey Research Laboratory, Univeristy of Illinois, Urbana.

Quigley, S., Steinkamp, M., Power, D., and Jones, B. 1978. Test of Syntactic Abilities. Dormac, Inc., Beaverton, Oregon.

Quigley, S., Wilbur, R., Power, D., Montanelli, D., and Steinkamp, M. 1976. Syntactic Structures in the Language of Deaf Children. Institute for Child Behavior and Development, Urbana, Illinois.

Rainer, J., and Altshuler, K. 1966. Comprehensive Mental Health Services for the Deaf. New York State Psychiatric Institute, Columbia University, New York.

Rawlings, B., and Jensema, C. 1977. Two Studies of the Families of Hearing Impaired Children. Series R., no. 5. Office of Demographic Studies, Gallaudet College, Washington, D.C.

Rawlings, B., and Trybus, R. 1978. Personnel, facilities and services available in schools and classes for hearing impaired children in the United States. Am. Ann. Deaf Directory of Programs and Service 123:99–114.

Ray, S. 1979. An adaption of the "Wechsler Intelligence Scale (Performance) for Children-Revised," Unpublished doctoral dissertation, University of Tennessee, Knoxville.

Richard, T., Triandes, H., and Patterson, C. 1963. Indices of employer prejudice toward disabled applicants. J. Applied Psychol. 47:52–55.

Rittenhouse, R. 1977. Horizontal decalage: The development of conservation in deaf students and the effect of the task instructions on their performance. Unpublished doctoral dissertation, University of Illinois, Urbana.

Robinson, L., and Weathers, O. 1974. Family therapy of deaf parents and hearing children. A new dimension in psychotherapeutic intervention. Am. Ann. Deaf 119:325–330.

Rogers, W., and Clarke, B. In press. Psychometric Characteristics of the Test of Syntactic Abilities Screening Test. Ed. Psychol. Meas.

Rosenstein, J. 1961. Perception, cognition, and language in deaf children. Except. Child. 27:276–284.

Ross, P., Pergament, L., and Anisfeld, M. 1979. Cerebral lateralization of deaf and hearing individuals for linguistic comparison judgments. Brain Lang. 8:69–80.

Russell, J. 1964. Reversal and nonreversal shift in deaf and hearing kindergarten children. Unpublished master's thesis, Catholic University of America, Washington, D.C.

Sachs, J. 1974. Memory in reading and listening to discourse. Mem. Cognit. 2:95–100.

Salem, J., and Herward, P. 1978. A survey to determine the impact of P.L. 94–142 on residential schools for the deaf. Am. Ann. Deaf 123:524–527.

Sarlin, M., and Altshuler, K. 1968. Group psychotherapy with deaf adolescents in a school setting. Int. J. Group Psychotherapy 18:337–344.

Schein, J., and Bushnaq, S. 1962. Higher education for the deaf in the United States: A retrospective investigation. Am. Ann. Deaf 107:416–420.

Schein, J., and Delk, M. 1974. The Deaf Population of the United States. National Association of the Deaf, Silver Spring, Maryland.

Schlesinger, H., and Meadow, K. 1972. Sound and Sign: Childhood Deafness and Mental Health. University of California Press, Berkeley.

Schlesinger, H., Geballe, C., Cotrell, A., and Leland, K. 1972. Language acquisition in four deaf children. In: H. Schlesinger and K. Meadow (eds.), Sound and Sign: Childhood Deafness and Mental Health. University of California Press, Berkeley.

Schlesinger, I. 1977. The role of cognitive development and linguistic input in language acquisition. J. Child Lang. 4:153–169.

Schlesinger, I., and Namir, L. (eds.). 1978. Sign Language of the Deaf. Academic Press, New York.

Simmons, A. 1962. A comparison of the type-token ratio of spoken and written language of deaf and hearing children. Volta Rev. 64:417–421.

Sinclair de Zwart, H. 1973. Language acquisition and cognitive development. In: T. Moore (ed.), Cognitive Development and the Acquisition of Language. Academic Press, New York.

Siple, P. (ed.). 1978. Understanding Language through Sign Language Research. Academic Press, New York.

Siple, P., Fischer, S., and Bellugi, U. 1977. Memory for nonsemantic attributes of American Sign Language signs and English words. J. Verb. Learn. Verb. Behav. 16:561–574.

Sisco, F., and Anderson, R. 1980. Deaf children's performance on the WISC-R relative to hearing status of parents and child rearing experiences. Am. Ann. Deaf 125:923–930.

Slobin, D. 1973. Cognitive prerequisites for the acquisition of grammar. In: C. Ferguson and D. Slobin (eds.), Studies of Child Language Development. Holt, Rinehart & Winston, Inc., New York.

Smith, L. 1972. The hard core Negro deaf adult in the Watts area of Los Angeles, California, J. Rehabil. Deaf 6:11–18.

Steinkamp, M., and Quigley, S. 1977. Assessing deaf children's written language. Volta Rev. 79:10–18.

Stinson, M. 1978. Effects of deafness or maternal expectations about child development. J. Spec. Ed. 12:75–81.

Stokoe, W. 1960. Sign language structure: An outline of the visual communication systems of the American deaf. Studies in Linguistics, Occasional Paper no. 8, reissued. Gallaudet College Press, Washington, D.C.

Stone, L. 1954. A critique of studies of infant isolation. Child Dev. 25:9–20.

Stuckless, R., and Birch, J. 1966. The influence of early manual communication on the linguistic development of deaf children. Am. Ann. Deaf 111:452–460, 499–504.

Stuckless, R., and Marks, C. 1966. Assessment of the Written Language of Deaf Students. University of Pittsburgh School of Education, Pittsburgh.

Sussman, A. 1973. An investigation into the relationship between self-concept of deaf adults and their perceived attitudes toward deafness. Unpublished doctoral dissertation, New York University.

Taylor, L. 1969. A language analysis of the writing of deaf children. Unpublished doctoral dissertation. Florida State University, Tallahassee.

Tomlinson-Keasey, C., and Kelly, R. 1978. The deaf child's symbolic world. Am. Ann. Deaf 123:452–459.

Trybus, R., and Karchmer, M. 1977. School achievement scores of hearing impaired children: National data on achievement status and growth patterns. Am. Ann. Deaf Directory of Programs and Services, 122:62–69.

Upshall, C. 1929. Day Schools vs. Institutions for the Deaf. Teachers College, Coumbia University, New York.

Uzgiris, I., and Hunt, J. 1975. Assessment in Infancy: Ordinal Scales of Psychological Assessment. University of Illinois Press, Urbana.

Vernon, M. 1967. Relationship of language to the thinking process. Arch. Gen. Psychol. 16:325–333.

Vernon, M., and Koh, S. 1970. Early manual communication and deaf children's achievement. Am. Ann. Deaf 115:527–536.

Virostek, S., and Cutting, J. 1979. Asymmetries for Ameslan handshapes and other forms in signers and nonsigners. Percept. Psychophys. 26:505–508.

Vogel, S. 1975. Syntactic Abilities in Normal and Dyslexic Children. University Park Press, Baltimore.

Wallace, G., and Corballis, M. 1973. Short-term memory and coding strategies of the deaf. J. Exper. Psych. 99:334–348.

Wampler, D. 1972. Linguistics of Visual English. Booklets, Santa Rosa, California.

Wedell-Monnig, J., and Lumley, J. 1980. Child deafness and mother-child interactions. Child Dev. 51:766–774.

WGBH-TV. The Caption Center. 1980. Readable English for Hearing Impaired Students. Linc Services, Inc., Boston, Massachusetts.

White, A., and Stevenson, V. 1975. The effects of total communication, manual communication, oral communication and reading on the learning of factual information in residential school deaf children. Am. Ann. Deaf 120:48–57.

Wilbur, R. 1979. American Sign Language and Sign Systems. University Park Press, Baltimore.

Wilbur, R., and Quigley, S. 1975. Syntactic structures in the written language of deaf children. Volta Rev. 77:194–203.

Wilbur, R., Montanelli, D., and Quigley, S. 1976. Pronomalization in the language of deaf students. J. Speech Hear. Res. 19:120–140.

Wilbur, R., Quigley, S., and Montanelli, D. 1975. Conjoined structures in the language of deaf students. J. Speech Hear. Res. 18:319–335.

Wilson, K. 1979. Inference and language processing in hearing and deaf children. Unpublished doctoral dissertation, Boston University.

Wolfram, W., and Fasold, R. 1974. The Study of Social Dialect in American English. Prentice-Hall, Inc., Englewood Cliffs, New Jersey.

Wrightstone, J., Aronow, M., and Moskowitz, S. 1963. Developing reading test norms for deaf children. Am. Ann. Deaf 108:311–316.

Youngs, J. 1975. Experiential deprivation: A response. Am. Ann. Deaf 120:553–554.

Youniss, J., and Furth, H. 1966a. Prediction of causal events as a function of transitivity and perceptual congruency in hearing and deaf children. Child Dev. 37:73–81.

Youniss, J., and Furth, H. 1966b. Spatial and temporal factors in learning with deaf children: An experimental investigation of thinking. Vocational Rehabilitation Administration Report RD–1305–S.

INDEX

Acoupedic (Unisensory) Method, 13, 14
Acquired hearing impairment, 3–4
Age, and hearing impairment, 3–4
American School for the Deaf, 38
American Sign Language (ASL), 12, 13,
    15–19, 25, 27, 36, 62, 79, 86,
    102, 104–105, 108–109
  antecedents of, 14
  children and, 16–19, 65–66
  description, 11
  as "natural" language, 25–26, 28
Ameslish (Pidgin Sign English), 18, 21,
    27–28, 104, 105, 108
  description, 13
Annual Survey of Hearing Impaired
    Children and Youth, 40, 43
ASL, see American Sign Language
Audiometer/audiogram, 2–3, 43
Auditory pure tone testing, 2–3
Auditory threshold, definition, 2
Aural/Oral Method, 13

Bonet, J., 14, 19

California State University, 7
Central hearing impairment, defini-
    tion, 3
Central Institute for the Deaf (CID),
    22–24, 68, 105
Childrearing practices, 87–89, 93, 101,
    see also Parents
CID, see Central Institute for the Deaf
Clarke School for the Deaf, 14, 22–24,
    105, 106
Clerc, L., 14, 28

Clinics, 7–8; see also specific clinics
Cognition
  deafness and, 50–60, 107
  language skills, 51–55
  of infants, 86
  see also Intelligence; Tests and
    testing
Columbia Presbyterian Hospital, 94
Conductive hearing impairment, defi-
    nition, 2
Conference of Milan (1880), 108
Congenital hearing impairment, 3–4
  and education, 17–19
Conservation behavior, 58–59
Crime, sexuality and, 94
Cued Speech, 20, 105, 108
  description, 12

"Deaf awareness," 102
Deafness
  definition, 4–5, 104
  incidence of, 5
  marriage and, 25
  see also Hearing impairment; Lan-
    guage skills; Tests and testing
Deaf Olympics, 99
de l'Éppée, C. M., 14, 15, 28, 38, 108

Education
  employment and, 98–99
  goal of, 103
  hearing status of children and,
    17–19, 101
  hearing status of parents and, 17–19
Employment, 95–99, 102

Fingerspelling, 19–20, 26, 60–61,
    79–81, 105
  description, 11
  Oral English methods and, 13, 14
Fraternal Society of the Deaf, 99
French Sign Language, 14

Gallaudet, T. H., 14, 28, 38
Gallaudet College, 7, 78
  Office of Demographic Studies
    (ODS), 40, 67–68, 85
Goldstein, M., 14
Green, F., 5

Health Examination Survey (1960,
    1963), 5
Health Interview Survey of Adults
    (1965, 1971), 5
Hearing impairment
  age at onset and, 3–4
  devices for, 66, 100, 108
  etiology, 4
  language skills and, 54–60
  measurement/classification of, 2–3,
    103–104
  types of, 3, 4, 43
  see also Deafness; Language skills;
    Tests and testing
Hearing threshold levels (HTL), 2–3
Heinicke, S., 14, 15, 108
HTL, see Hearing threshold levels
Hereditary hearing impairment, 3–4
Homosexuality, 101

Illinois School for the Deaf, 46
Impulsivity, 91–92
Infants
  cognitive development of, 86
  institutionalization of, 32–33
  language skills and, 10
Institutionalization
  definition, 31
  impact of, 32
  mental retardation and, 32–33
  see also Schools
Intelligence, 27, 83, 84, 92
  testing of, 34, 56
  vocational planning and, 98
  see also Cognition

John Tracy Clinic, 8

Langley Porter Hospital, 94
Language skills
  American Sign Language and, 15–19
  cognition and, 51–54
  hearing impairment and, 54–60
  infants and, 10
  Manual English and, 19–22
  Oral English and, 22–24
  see also Reading; Writing; specific
    languages
Learned helplessness, 90–92
Leisure, 99–100
Lexington School for the Deaf, 105
Linguistics of Visual English (LOVE), 12
Lipreading, 12
  Cued Speech and, 20

Mainstreaming, 37–38, 42–47, 106
  antecedents to, 38–39
  criteria for, 44
  mental retardation and, 39
  problems in, 46
  regional programs for, 45–47,
    106–107
Manual English, 19–22, 25, 27, 28, 86
  Cued Speech, 20, 105, 108
    description, 12
  Fingerspelling, 13, 14, 19–20, 26,
    60–61, 79–81, 105
    description, 11
  Linguistics of Visual English (LOVE),
    12
  Pidgin Sign (Ameslish, Siglish), 13,
    18, 21, 27–28, 104, 105, 108
  reading and, 76, 86
  Seeing Essential English (SEE-I), 14,
    20–21
    description, 12
  Signed English, 21, 77–78
    description, 13
  Signing Exact English (SEE-II), 14,
    21, 28, 104, 105, 108
    description, 12–13
Marriage, 101
  deafness and, 25
Mediation, symbolic, 59, 60–63, 78–81
Memory, syntactic skills and, 80–81
Mental health, 93–94

Mental retardation
    institutionalization and, 32–33
    mainstreaming and, 39
Mills v. Board of Education (1972), 39
Mixed loss, definition, 3

National Association of the Deaf
    (NAD), 99
National Health Survey, 5
National Speech and Hearing Survey
    (1968–1969), 5
National Technical Institute for the
    Deaf, 7, 78
Neo-Oralism, 105
Northwestern Syntax Screening Test
    (NSST), 21, 23

ODS, *see* Office of Demographic
    Studies, Gallaudet College
Office of Demographic Studies (ODS),
    Gallaudet College, 40, 67–68,
    85
Oral English, 22–24, 25, 27, 104–105
    Acoupedic (Unisensory) Method, 14
    description, 13
    Aural/Oral Method, 13
    fingerspelling and, 13, 14
    reading and, 76, 86
    schools and, 27–28
    use of, with children, 19
Oral Method, 13
    compared with Rochester Method, 20
    early use of, 14–15

Parents
    childrearing practices of, 87–89, 93,
        101
    hearing status of, 15–19, 25–26, 34,
        36, 40, 61, 87–89, 101, 105
    interaction with deaf children, 34–35
*Pennsylvania Association for Retarded
    Citizens (PARC) v. Common-
    wealth of Pennsylvania* (1971),
    39
Personality, development of, in deaf
    children, 90–92
Pidgin Sign English (Ameslish, Siglish),
    13, 18, 21, 27–28, 104, 105, 108
PL94-142, *see* Public Law 94-142

Ponce de Léon, P., 14
Postlingual hearing impairment, 4, 43
Prejudice, 99
    of employers, 94, 102
    racial, 100
Prelingual hearing impairment, 4,
    103–104
Psychosocial development, childrearing
    practices and, 87–89, 93, 101
Public Law (PL) 94-142 (1975), 39, 45
Pure tone average (PTA), 2

*Readable English for the Hearing Im-
    paired Student* (WGBH Cap-
    tioning Center), 78
Reading, 103–104
    academic achievement and, 84–86,
        107–108
    deaf children and, 66–81
        achievement levels, 67–69, 76–77
        measurement difficulties, 69–77
    factors affecting, 45
    inner language and, 78–81
    as leisure activity, 100
    Manual English and, 76, 86
    materials for teaching of, 66–67,
        70–73, 77–78
    Oral English and, 76, 86
    short-term memory (STM) and,
        80–81, 86
    symbolic mediation and, 60–63
    syntactic difficulties in, 69–78
    written language and, 81–82
    see also Language skills; Writing
Reading for Meaning, 70–73
Reading Milestones, 78
Rochester Institute of Technology, 7
Rochester Method, 13, 14, 22, 105
    compared with Oral Method, 20
Rochester School for the Deaf, 14
Rockland State Hospital, 94

St. Elizabeth Hospital, 94
St. Joseph's Institute for the Deaf, 22,
    24
St. Joseph's School for the Deaf, 105,
    106
Schizophrenia, 94
Schools, 6
    attendance of, 7

Schools—*continued*
  day, 37, 105–106
    compared to residential, 39–42
    Oral English in, 27–28
    self-concept in, 92
    social maturity and, 93
  establishment of, 5
  institutionalization and, 31–33
  mainstreaming and, 38–39, 42–47
  number of, in the U.S., 5–7
  residential, 37, 105–106
    antecedents to, 38
    compared to day, 39–42
    self-concept in, 92
    sexuality and, 101
    social maturity and, 93
  see also specific schools
SEE-I, *see* Seeing Essential English
SEE-II, *see* Signing Exact English
Seeing Essential English (SEE-I), 14,
    20–21
  description, 12
Self-perception, 91–92
Sensorineural hearing impairment,
    definition, 3
Seriation, 58
Sexuality, 100–102
  crime and, 94
Short-term memory (STM), 80–81, 86
Sicard, R. A., 14, 28, 38
Siglish (Pidgin Sign English), 18, 21,
    27–28, 104, 105, 108
  description, 13
Signed English, 21, 77–78
  description, 13
Signing Exact English (SEE-I), 14, 21,
    28, 104, 105, 108
  description, 12–13
Sign language
  language development and, 35
  see also American Sign Language;
    French Sign Language; Manual
    English
*Sign Language Structure: An Outline
  of the Visual Communication
  Systems of the American Deaf,*
  16
Simultaneous Method, *see* Total Communication
Social adjustment, 92–93, 99–102
  in residential v. day schools, 41–42

Sound, physical parameters of, 2
*Special Edition for the Hearing
  Impaired* of the *SAT,* 85
Speech
  of day v. residential students, 40–42
  fingerspelling and, 19
Speechreading, 12, 13, 19, 26, 40
Stanford Achievement Test, 21, 23, 67,
    68, 69, 84, 85
Status, economic/occupational, 95–99
Symbolic thought, 59, 60–63, 78–81

Telecommunications device (TTY), 100
Test of Syntactic Abilities (TSA), 21,
    70, 71, 78
TSA Syntax Program, 78
Tests and testing
  Alpern-Boll Developmental Profile,
    36
  audiometer/audiogram, 2–3, 43
  Carrow Elicited Language Inventory,
    23
  Developmental Sentence Analysis, 23
  *Meadow/Kendall Social Emotional
    Assessment Inventory,* 41
  Metropolitan Achievement Test, 67
  Northwestern Syntax Screening Test
    (NSST), 21, 23
  Peabody Picture Vocabulary Test, 21
  Raven's Progressive Matrices, 51
  Stanford Achievement Test, 21, 23,
    67, 68, 69, 84, 85
  Test of Syntactic Abilities (TSA),
    20, 70, 71, 78
  Vineland Social Maturity Scale (the
    Vineland), 92–93
  *Wechsler Intelligence Scale of Chil-
    dren* (WISC), 56
  *Wechsler Intelligence Scale for Chil-
    dren—Revised* (WISC-R), 34, 56
  Wide-Span Reading Test, 68
  Woodworth and Wells Test, 67
Texas State School for the Deaf, 47
Total Communication (Simultaneous
    Method), 13, 14–15, 22, 27, 28,
    35, 37, 105, 108
  definition, 26
  parent-child interactions and, 35–36
  reading and, 76
Transitive thinking, 58–59

TSA, *see Test of Syntactic Abilities*
Tucker-Maxon School, 105

Unemployment, *see* Employment
University of Nebraska—Lincoln, 78

Videotaping, of American Sign Language, 66
Vineland Social Maturity Scale (the Vineland), 92–93
Vocational maturity, 97–98

Wechsler Intelligence Scale for Children (WISC), 56
Wechsler Intelligence Scale for Children—Revised (WISC-R), 34, 56
Whorfian hypothesis
strong form, 52–53
weak form, 53
Whorfian-Sapir hypothesis, 54
WISC, *see Wechsler Intelligence Scale for Children*
WISC-R, *see Wechsler Intelligence Scale for Children—Revised*
Writing, 81–86
academic achievement and, 84–86
see also Language skills; Reading